Tellin' It for the Truth

To Linda & Jim!

Tellin' It
for the Truth

Dec. 17, 2013

By Bill Landry

Bill Landry

Celtic Cat Publishing

KNOXVILLE, TENNESSEE

Celtic Cat Publishing
2654 Wild Fern Lane,
Knoxville, Tennessee 37931
www.celticcatpublishing.net
www.celticcatpublishing.com

Manufactured in the United States of America
Book and cover design: Dariel Mayer

Publisher's Cataloging-in-Publication Data
Landry, Bill.
Tellin' It for the Truth / Bill Landry.
p. cm.
ISBN: 978-0-9847836-4-9 (pbk.)
ISBN: 978-0-9891380-1-7 (hardcover)
1. Tennessee—Social life and customs. 2. Great
Smoky Mountains (N.C. and Tenn.)—Social life and
customs.
I. Title.
F440 .L361 2013
976.8—dc23
2013935008

From Chattanooga to Bristol, and in honor of
Douglas D. Mills, into southern Kentucky;
from the Great Smoky Mountains to Cookeville
and all parts in between; thank you to the good people
of East Tennessee, for your friendships, help,
and continuous support throughout my life.
This book is dedicated to you, you-all.

Contents

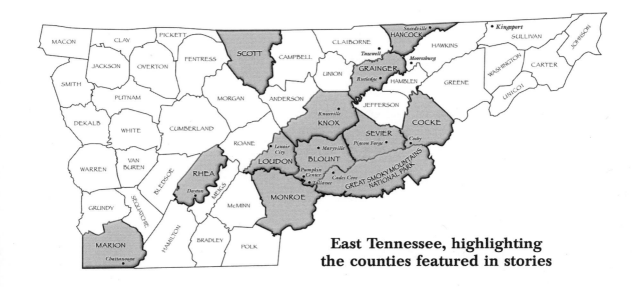

East Tennessee, highlighting the counties featured in stories

Preface

When a good story is told and retold, it's usually because there's a lot of truth connected with it.

When someone says that the story they're about to tell is true or that they're "tellin' it for the truth," it usually means something good is coming.

"Tellin' it for the truth" also means that the storyteller wants us to know that the story is true as far as the storyteller knows, so we should believe it. It might also mean that the story was told *as if* it were true, so we can feel good about retelling it.

These are some of my favorite stories that I'm tellin' for the truth. They're Bill's stories because I'm telling them—they're from my experiences. But they're also everyone's stories—they're about who we are and what we're doing here.

There's an adventure, some history, an Olympic memory, a football recollection, a love story, and a tragic tale. Some are personal. Some are historical. Some are comical. Some are sorrowful. Most are somewhere in between.

You can believe them because they are true, and tell them again if you like. Oh, there's some embellishment in them, some exaggeration, but they're stories! They ought to be fun. So, like Ray Hicks says, "You can tell it any ole way and it's still the truth."

I'm pleased to share them with you. Publicly, I want to acknowledge the debt of gratitude and thanks I owe my publisher, editor, and friend, Jim Johnston, for compiling these stories into a book so you can read them.

Some I've waited many years to tell. They're all true except "The Ballad of Pirate Paddy O'Dea." Now, that one isn't true, for I made it up. The transition jokes or tales aren't true either. They're "tales." Everything else, all the stories, are true. I promise.

That's what these are: stories worth telling and hearing or reading. They are worth my time to write them, your time to read them and even tell them again, if you want. It's like the title Hawthorne gave his book: *Twice Told Tales*, stories told and told again. That's what I'm all about.

Hopefully, you'll feel the same way, for I've got a theory about storytelling: all good stories once told are told again.

Bill Landry
Summer 2013

The Spartans of Rhea County

Prologue

This is one of the more dramatic tales of the region. It involves a little-known bunch of girls. Actually, they were a band of war heroes who called themselves the "Spartans of Rhea County." They were brave women, and their heroic actions in defense of their families and community should be remembered.

When referring to the Civil War, one rarely hears the term "sister against sister." Of course, East Tennessee was torn apart—divided loyalties and all that. But when we hear and read about the Civil War, it's usually a male thing. We rarely hear tales about heroic women, and that's why this story has stuck with me.

The story would make a great movie. One of the Spartans, Rhoda Tennessee Thomison, could be portrayed by a young Winona Rider or Kiera Knightly, and perhaps Reese Witherspoon as Minerva. In the film, Rhoda might even fall in love with one of the boys who becomes her captor. We don't know this actually happened. With so many women in the club and the local boys off to war or in hiding, the young Union soldiers were all that was available. It's not beyond the realm of possibility.

Heroines of the Civil War

The story begins in Rhea County, Tennessee, near Dayton, the place where the Scopes Monkey Trial took place. It's about halfway between Knoxville and Chattanooga. Today, it's about an hour's drive by car from either place. During the Civil War, it would have taken perhaps three days on horseback. For an army on the march, it might have taken a week. During the war, the communities of that area were known as Washington (the county seat) and Smith's Crossroads.

It didn't take long for Tennessee to feel the ravages of war.

First, the Confederates came through like a swarm of locusts and devoured everything. The Yankees followed on their heels, taking everything of value that was left. By 1863, most of the state, including East Tennessee, was devastated. The Union army, traveling northeast up the Tennessee Valley from Chattanooga toward Knoxville, passed through Smith's Crossroads. Troops were on the move before and after the battles of Chickamauga, Chattanooga, and Missionary Ridge, as well as Grant's victory at Lookout Mountain.

The region abounds with stories of family heirloom silver being dug up and stolen, of work animals hidden from one army only to be found and eaten by the other, and rail fences burned for warmth.

We grew up hearing about these stories and events, not so much from history books, but from our own families. Around East Tennessee, history is personal. My great, great grandfather, for instance, fought for the Confederates. He entered the war as a sergeant and came out a major. He was wounded at Vicksburg and Shiloh and finished the war in a Mobile hospital.

War harms a place and wounds a region. Through the sheer numbers involved, as it passes through an area like a destructive wave, an army tends to bully the populace. Then, guerrilla bands often fill the void that is left. Communities struggle for law and order. Without it, roaming marauders, or "bushwhackers," as they were called, scour the region, attack the defenseless, murder local folks, and steal what they can.

During the Civil War, those at home or back from war, even those not involved in the fighting, suffered. The populace, the home-front folks, were just your average Tennesseans – if there is such a thing. Most were struggling just to survive, hanging on as best they could.

More soldiers from Tennessee died fighting for the Union army during the Civil War than from all but three Union states. And more Tennessee soldiers died fighting for the Confederate army than from all but two other Southern states. Tennessee paid the price for that horrible war: Tennesseans died by the thousands because so many battles were fought here. In 1840, Tennessee was known as "The Hog and Hominy State," but during the Civil War, its great sacrifices helped earned it the moniker, "The Volunteer State." Armies didn't just pass through; they fought. They stayed and wintered here, because this is where the food was, particularly during the winters of 1862 and 1863. That's why the war did so much damage, and that's why we always hear about Tennessee feeding both armies during the Civil War, because it's true.

And while not too much has been written about "sister against sister," the stories of the women who lived through it all are worth telling. This is one of those stories, and it's true.

Our story begins with a rousing chorus of "hizzah's," amidst the swelled chests, boyish smiles, rosy cheeks, and sunny faces of soldier boys marching off to a war that is just beginning. Of course, like the rest of the country, our young Tennessee soldiers were full of themselves. They were all puffed up and full of bearded oaths and pride, certain that soon they would be performing heroic deeds and actions. They hadn't yet come face-to-face, "even unto the cannon's mouth," as the great bard described the scene in a different battle.

But it's not the boys of Rhea County, smack dab in the middle of East Tennessee, which concern us in this story. It's their childhood sweethearts and their sisters. In and around Smith's Crossroads, at the beginning of the Civil War, a group of young girls aged fifteen to seventeen decided to form a club.

They came from the surrounding large farms. At first, they met regularly at the elegant homes of some of the girls, for most of them were from the more affluent families. They brought their sisters and their cousins, too. Many had older brothers already in companies, while others had brothers approaching enlistment age. They all wanted to do their part to help the cause, and their cause was the Confederate one. The girls named their club "The Spartans."

Barbara Allen's father, for instance, would be in a Yankee prison, three of her brothers would be with Gen. Robert E. Lee, and another brother with Gen. Joseph E. Johnston. Rhoda Thomison had one brother who would be wounded at Shiloh, one killed at Chickamauga, and one would be with with Gen. Lee.

Barbara Allen

The unique thing about Dayton, Tennessee and its environs—what set it apart from other East Tennessee counties—is that Rhea County had Southern leanings. Like only a few other East Tennessee counties, such as Polk, Monroe, Meigs, and Sullivan, Rhea County was Confederate. Naturally, so were the Spartans.

As the war continued and times grew harsher and more desperate, the young ladies quit having teas and playing cards and chose to put away their board games. They yearned to do more to help their families and the war effort—to do their part. They made a conscious decision to act, to make more of a contribution. Just because they were female was no reason they couldn't participate. They were excellent horsewomen, so they utilized their talents and incorporated them into their meeting rituals and duties by forming a cavalry. Add to this courage, ingenuity, and determination: they had a mission to assist the Confederate war effort, and they couldn't be kept from it. As the war progressed, the Spartans, our young ladies, began to undertake a more adult role in their community, a community that was being occupied by the enemy.

Rhea County had already produced seven Confederate companies and only one for the Union. The Spartans formed what would become the only female cavalry company in the war. They elected Mary McDonald, captain; Caroline McDonald, her sister-in-law, 1st lieutenant; Anne Paine, 2nd lieutenant; and Rhoda Tennessee Thomison, 3rd lieutenant. These were the officers of the newly ordained female cavalry. "Side-Saddle Soldiers," they called themselves. History even records their non-commissioned officers, thanks to an article written in 1911 by William G. Allen for *Confederate Veterans* magazine. They were: Jane Keith, 1st sergeant; Rachael Howard, 2nd sergeant; Sallie Mitchell, 3rd sergeant; and Minerva Torches, 4th sergeant. The rest of the ladies were all privates: Barbara Allen, Josephine Allen, Sidney McDonald, Maggie Keith, Mary Paine, Jane Locke, Mary Robinson, Louisa McDonald, Sarah Rudd, Mary Anne McDonald, and Margaret Sykes.

3rd Lieutenant Rhoda
Tennessee Thomison

While Union regiments and cavalry continued moving up from Chattanooga into their community, the Spartans' activities began simply enough. They cut and collected bandages from rags and sheets, rolled them, and administered them to the wounded. They scoured the forests for medicinal plants, nursed the injured, baked bread and other foods to feed their brothers and fathers in the field. It is perhaps on one of these assignments that we can envision the girls astride their horses, high on a wind-blown hill. Below, exhausted, yet determined, Longstreet's army is trudging onward, northeast. The young Spartans may even have ridden down and met the great General himself, lifting his men's spirits at just the sight of this determined feminine band.

By the summer of 1863, Union General Ambrose Burnside entered East Tennessee. This marked a turning point for the girls. In order to continue their clandestine operations, they were forced to hold their meetings in abandoned rural churches. As the Union Army gained more complete control of the region, Confederate sympathizers became less outspoken and, in time, they went underground altogether. By December 1864, the last Southern stronghold in East Tennessee finally fell. Federal troops gained full control of Rhea County.

Meanwhile, with an abundance of Union soldiers around, it's easy to understand their attraction to the local girls and vice versa. With so many young men forced away from home for the first time, the soldiers probably had eyes for the pretty Rhea County girls. That's another reason the pot was beginning to boil, as they say, and in more ways than one! After all, the Union sol-

General
James Longstreet

General
Ambrose Burnside

Civil War Troop Movements

diers were teenagers, too—young adults with all the passions and "young man's fancy." The soldiers were homesick and lonely, so the Spartans were no doubt very appealing to them. After all, the Spartans were the prettiest girls and from the best families in the county. The Union soldiers would understandably be drawn to the girls.

The older, self-proclaimed wiser members of our feminine club used this to their advantage. It became part of their mission and purpose. With expertise in the use of feminine wiles, they began to accumulate information on troop movements, where food and ammunition stores were kept, and the like. In time, the Spartans actively engaged in the war effort as full-fledged spies for the South.

Intrigues developed as husbands couldn't return to visit their homes and families. With communities occupied by the enemy, it was far too dangerous. What started out as harmlessly getting a message to Daddy soon evolved into smuggling and espionage activities. Mary Paine wrote cryptically worded letters to her brother Hannibal, using terms like "candy stew" as a form of code. (Its meaning is still unclear.) Furthermore, their girlish underground cloak-and-dagger escapades began to have a pronounced effect upon the Federals, if not wreaking havoc upon Union control of East Tennessee.

The situation was tenuous. By the spring of 1865, matters worsened when a local farmer, described in records as having a complete personal worth of $180 and some land, began to make it his mission to capture and destroy the Spartans. Our antagonist had managed to dodge Confederate conscription for years. Historical records describe him as a typical draft dodger who waited until the war was decided before joining the Union so that he could share in the spoils. His name was Captain John Walker.

Walker succeeded in gathering about him a rag-tag group to replace the disbanded 6th Tennessee mounted infantry. The regiment, named "Goon's Hog Back Regulars," was organized with Walker as captain. It was described as being no better than other nameless guerilla bands flourishing in the region at the time. The difference, however, was that Walker's band of brigands operated with the full knowledge of the occupiers. He had both power and authority over the entire community, a dangerous combination. Besides, he was a Union Captain of the 6th Tennessee mounted infantry in charge of Rhea County.

One of Walker's first acts was to order the arrest of the Spartans. Walker convinced his superior, Lt. Col. George Gowin of Hamilton County, to let him go after the women. This occurred at the same time that Robert E. Lee was making his final desperate march toward Appomattox. Walker had endured ridicule from the Spartans' families in the past. Now, in his position of authority, he was going to arrest the Rhea County Spartans, all of them! Nobody was going to stop him. To hell with the fact they were women and girls.

On the night of April 5, 1865, Walker sent his men after the Spartans. First, he planned to round up the leaders. Captain Mary McDonald and her sister-in-law, Caroline, were the first to be arrested. Third Lieutenant Rhoda Tennessee Thomison was arrested the next day at her home. Her father, a retired Confederate soldier, was present. Throughout the county, this pogrom continued. Seven others, accused of being Spartans, were arrested, roughly treated, and their horses were confiscated. They were forced to march over five miles to Bell's Landing on the Tennessee River. Soon, all of the other Spartans were marched miles across the county in the rain and brought to join their officers.

On the banks of the Tennessee River, in mud up to their pretty knees, the Spartans were assembled. The USS Chattanooga waited to take them to Chattanooga for trial and possible execution. The riverboat, ordered built by General Ulysses S. Grant as a supply vessel, was a nasty hog- and cattle-carrying paddle-wheeler. It plied its trade on the Upper Tennessee when navigable waters permitted. The USS Chattanooga was the riverboat's Federal name. The locals living along the river knew it as "The Chicken Thief," the same vessel that stole their produce, animals, and valuables and hauled them downriver. There were no rooms or beds for the Spartans aboard the dingy vessel. They were thrown into one area, oldest to youngest, and forced to sleep on the floor, with guards posted to prevent their escape.

Wet and caked in mud, the bedraggled Spartans appeared defeated. But, like all the great avengers of oppression in fact and fiction—in the grand tradition of the Swamp Fox, the Scarlet Pimpernel, and Batman—though things certainly looked bleak for our brave ladies, yet there was hope. Though they sure were in a tight spot, they had been in tight spots before. Things were not quite hopeless. After all, they were still alive.

Upon arriving in Chattanooga, the Spartans were promptly marched under guard seven blocks down Market Street. Their captors orchestrated this spectacle as a warning to others and to further ridicule and embarrass the ladies. They headed to the provost marshal's office, to be brought before the officer in charge of the Union occupying force.

Upon reaching the provost's office, they were met by Captain Seth Moe, who greeted Walker and immediately sent for his commander, Major General James Stedman. Finally, after days of marching through mud and rain and enduring a rough-and-

Chattanooga river bluffs

tumble riverboat trip aboard a mangy craft, our heroines found themselves standing face-to-face with the enemy General. They were about to face their destiny.

As we near the end of our story, it's not impossible that a full-blown Romeo-and-Juliet-like love affair has developed. Our leading Spartan lass, perhaps, has fallen madly in love with a handsome young Union 1st lieutenant, possibly a certain Lieutenant William Gothard, one of Walker's unfortunate underlings.

Historically speaking, Gothard was actually known to the girls and probably liked.

Evidence exists that Captain Mary McDonald, fearful of mistreatment by Captain Walker, wrote to Walker's superior officer requesting that Lieutenant Gothard accompany the women to Chattanooga. But the request was refused.

In this drama, perhaps our love-struck lieutenant's responsibility was to guard and bring the women to Chattanooga. And, sadly, to watch as their pretty necks were stretched way more than they ever had been before. Anyway, Lt. Gothard probably did accompany them, and that's our subplot, this Capulet/Montague romance thing going on.

Entering and standing beside Captain Moe (Curley, Larry, and . . .), the General is a gruff, cigar-chewing type, possibly a veteran of bloody Chickamauga. He is facing Captain Mary Mc-Donald, the obvious leader of the band of brigands.

All the Spartans are present, possibly tied up or shackled by their antagonist, the nasty Union Captain Walker. Walker no doubt is extremely proud of himself at this moment. He has un-covered their plot to save the Confederacy, to undermine his authority, or at the very least to get food and information to their fathers, brothers, and uncles.

This is obviously the climax of our movie, a historical biopic full of the facts of the actual events. But what does the future hold for Captain Mary, our heroine, and her love-struck lieutenant? Sadly, she foresees it, too: her lover faces the very real possibility of having to hang his own fiancé: specifically, of having to put a rope around her neck, instead of a ring on her finger. Yikes! But, that can't happen, or can it? Did it?

The truth is, as they say, stranger than fiction. For in this story things actually do work out for the best, and everyone does end up living happily ever after. Well, at least as happily as folks could live in ravaged, war-torn East Tennessee following the Civil War, where most communities and survivors didn't have seed corn, much less anything else to eat.

So here's the climactic scene:

General James Stedman, having been well versed in the crimes the Spartans are accused of committing, is standing in front of the girls. Facing him is the smirking, oily, supercilious Captain Walker, who continues his accusations. He's proud of himself for having bested this bunch of traitorous scoundrels masquerading as brave, innocent, and helpless women – well, maybe not so in-nocent, and certainly not so helpless either! So, Captain Walker, with great finality and aplomb, finishes his accusations.

There is a pause.

The camera captures close-ups of all the principal characters, revealing simply each participant's position in the conflict. We know which side they are on and that the Captain is a real ass. The General looks at each female traitor's face before him.

There is another dramatic pause.

Then, General Stedman promptly orders Captain Walker to

Mocasin Bend 1902

"get these girls cleaned up!" He orders Walker to immediately find rooms for them in Chattanooga's finest Central House Hotel; to take them to the city's finest restaurant to get them fed; and to return them unharmed, with the government's complete apology, to their homes in Rhea County.

General Stedman rages against Walker's actions and calls them "foolishness." The General apologizes to the women for Walker's behavior, saying, "Not all Yankees are barbarians." He adds, harshly, "And, if one hair is harmed on any of these girls' heads and I hear about it, there will be more than a little hell to pay. Do you understand me, Captain?" Further, he disbands Captain Walker's 6th Tennessee mounted infantry.

Epilogue

Walker did return the Rhea County Spartans upriver, but not to the women's homes as ordered. Instead, he left them on the riverbank, forcing them to get home any way they could. They walked. On the trip back to Rhea County, the girls learned of Lee's surrender. After the war, Walker managed to find a few petty local political appointments. Then, he slipped into obscurity.

As to whether any of the Spartans married any of the handsome Union soldiers, I don't know. Whether or not these brave Rhea County Civil War heroines actually did live happily ever after, we can only hope.

When the story of the Spartans was first told and printed in 1911, there remained only three members still alive: Mary McDonald, Mary Ann McDonald, and Third Lieutenant Rhoda Tennessee Thomison.

Today, in and around Rhea County, Tennessee, the McDonald name is still held in high regard. In Chattanooga, the name McDonald is associated with the old *Chattanooga News Free Press.* In fact, I went to school with a Louise 'Weezie' Davenport, who might even be a relative to the McDonalds in Chattanooga where I grew up. Hey, she was my first girlfriend. I was in the third grade. Come to think of it, she was a real pistol, too. I wouldn't be surprised if her great, great, grandmother turned out to be Captain Mary McDonald, herself—Mary McDonald, member of the Side-Saddle Soldiers, the Spartans of Rhea County, the only female cavalry on either side in the Civil War.

One final note: General Stedman did ask that each member of the Spartans take the oath of allegiance to the United States, which they did.

Dr. Calvin Dickenson, Professor of History, Tennessee Tech University, and his co-author, Jennie Ivey, tell this story in their work, *Soldiers, Spies, and Spartans,* as well. So, I'm not completely making this up. I'm tellin' it for the truth.

Buddy: Dog of the Smoky Mountains

The phone rings.

"Hello. Is this the owner of Buddy, a brown and white dog who lives near the Smoky Mountains? I'm calling the phone number on his collar. You might want to know that your dog is at the trail head of Abrams Creek Falls in Cades Cove."

"Is he brown and white and real friendly?"

"Yeah, that's him. He's about the coolest dog I've ever seen. He's standing there at the beginning of the trailhead just greeting everybody. He's *real* friendly. Somebody's going to take him home. I thought about it myself. You better go get him before the rangers do. Buddy's sure one cool dog."

"Thank you. Glad you called."

"No need to thank me. Goodbye."

People love their dogs. It's like a mother loves her children or a hen her chicks. Of course she does! A good dog will bring out the best in someone, usually its owner. "I wish I could be the person my dog thinks I am" is a sentimental saying, but true. Every dog-gone dog owner knows it, too. It's something to strive towards.

I want to tell you about my dog. Many people know him. In fact, more people know Buddy than know me, and I'm on TV.

Buddy is wanted. He's a habitual criminal. He just can't help it. I know you've heard that before—that's what they all say. In prison, everybody is innocent, according to the warden. I'm sorry to say it's true: Bud's not innocent. Bud's wanted by the park rangers, the Cades Cove Visitor's Center folks, and the backcountry rangers. His arrest warrants look like this:

United States District Court Violation Notice
Place of offense: Cades Cove Backcountry,
Abrams Falls Trail.

DOG OFF LEASH
BILL LANDRY

You must pay amount indicated below or appear in court.
Forfeiture Amount: $50.00 + $25.00 Processing Fee
$75.00 Total Collateral Due

BUSTED AGAIN! For you innocents, non-hunters, and rookies, "Forfeiture Amount" is what it costs you (actually, what it costs me!). It's the fine for a dog getting caught in the National Park without a leash. Buddy has a rap sheet a mile long.

Ranger Edna McNutt at the Cades Cove Visitor's Center knows most of the crimes Buddy has ever committed. She reports that he'll just walk into the Visitor's Center and nonchalantly act like everyone else. The ranger on duty will look up and ask the people in front of and behind Buddy, "Is that your dog?"

Quickly, they'll respond with a fervent "No!" or "I never saw him before in my life, Officer!" Then, they'll slide over to get as far away as possible from Buddy and the Forfeiture Amount. They want to be sure the ranger knows they are not part of Buddy's gang.

He doesn't look like a criminal. That's why he's so successful. Often, until just last year, he would go hiking with whoever

Buddy playing by Abrams sign

J.D.'s photo of Buddy

was traveling the five-mile distance from Abrams Creek Campground to Abrams Falls. The hikers then would go into Cades Cove from Abrams Falls, and Buddy would naturally follow along, too.

That's where he repeatedly got into trouble. You see, when the hikers finish the trail, they get in their cars and go home. Buddy, on the other hand, goes to jail. Bingo! Ca Ching! It was costing us a fortune. We were desperate enough to consider an invisible fence. But we didn't think Buddy, if he were chasing a bear or other critter, would stop and consider waiting at the invisible fence line.

J.D. Schandt of Trail Hard sent me a nice thank-you note for Buddy. It demonstrates what I mean. Buddy has a secret other life. He's a thru-hiker and a trainer of wilderness wanderers like himself. J.D. says:

> *I have hiked with Buddy on three occasions. I climbed the three Cascades in Washington this summer and Buddy was instrumental in my training for the climbs. Have you ever tried to keep up with him on Rabbit Creek Trail? He's a machine! The above pictures were taken in December 2011. We hiked 21 miles from Abrams Ranger Station to Parson's Branch Road and back. Buddy led all the way. 9/25/12*

Laying low in the flowers, cooling it

For a while last year, every time the rangers spotted Buddy they would bust him. Of course, he wasn't allowed in the Park, and they were doing their jobs. But, the Budro couldn't help it. He spent many a night in the slammer during those wild days of his youth.

He's grown up some now. He's just over two years old. But, wait a minute! Doesn't that make him a teenager in people years? Oh no! Now we've got to look forward to a teenage Buddy. Yikes!

Buddy has been busted more than a few times. All right, maybe more than a dozen times. Okay, maybe many dozens! The problem is that Buddy, for all his innate intelligence and wily street smarts, can't read. I guess he dropped out in the second quarter of doggie day care.

But, you can't really blame a dog for being a dog. What's he supposed to do—act like an opossum or a chicken? He's a dog. Sometimes I wish he were a person, and sometimes he actually acts like my cousin, Kevin. But, no, he's a "d-o-g."

If you lived right next to the National Park and your nearest neighbor was half-a-mile away, would you keep your dog on a leash? It's difficult. I've tried. First of all, it could be a death sentence, because coyotes or bears might get him. Secondly, Buddy, by nature, is a gregarious salesman. He'll look at you with those big, sad browns, and you'll just melt and fork over whatever you have on you.

Other times, he'll just act like anybody else. In summer, usually all he wants to do is go down to Abrams Creek and take a swim. While there, sure he's looking for a hug and a hot dog just like everyone else. You can't blame him; I want the same, don't you?

Thirdly, it can be lonely living in the mountains, even if you're next to a national park. Imagine you're a dog and you hear happy children squealing and tubers tubing and riding the white water of Abrams Creek. This type of activity tends to attract a fun-loving, people-person dog like the Budro.

Once, after he went missing for two days, we finally got a phone call. It was from a nice family of four. As cell phones don't work in the Park, they were calling from back home in West Knoxville.

"Do you have a brown and white dog named Buddy?"

Elated, we responded, "DO we?" He's actually a Walker hound, about 60 pounds, but the breed he most represents and aspires to is Human.

Anyway, the caller continued: "Did you lose your dog?" Interesting question, I thought to myself. "Did I lose my dog" isn't the question. The question is "Did someone TAKE my dog from the Abrams Creek area?" But, I didn't say that. I said, "Yes, Buddy is our dog and YES, he went missing two days ago. Have you seen him?"

This brought a long pause, and then a sense of sadness to the caller's voice. He explained that when they left the National Park campground, since Buddy had played with their two children for two days, they thought he was lost and wanted him to have a good home. But, Buddy already has a pretty good home. We don't feed him steaks every day, but he's relatively happy here, I think.

After driving an hour into Knoxville, I met these fine people at Moe's Restaurant on Northshore Drive. It was like a wake, a tragedy of titanic proportions. "Oh, Buddy, we love you," the seven-year-old little boy wailed. His nine-year-old sister blubbered, "Buddy is the best dog in the whole world! Why can't we keep him, Mama? Can't we keep him? Pleeeease!"

I wanted to take control of the situation and say, "No, you can't keep him. You shouldn't have taken him, you goofy people." But I thought to myself, keep quiet!

Buddy has that effect on people. He disrupts you emotionally. Then, just when you're at your weakest, he looks at you with those big brown eyes, and he's gotcha. You fork it over, whatever you've got: a hot dog, half a hamburger, a cracker, your heart. If you've got nothing, he'll nuzzle up for a head scratch, a butt scratch, anything he wants. You're in his power now.

A few months ago, my wife finally had a new collar made for The Bud Man. It not only gave his name and our phone number, but we added another sentence: "Buddy knows his way home." It's helped a lot.

There was a time when a collar on a dog meant it had a home—you can't take it. A collar was enough to exact a call from most good-hearted Samaritans who think they've "found" a dog. They don't understand; Buddy's found *them.* Don't they get it?

If there were enough room, my wife would have added: "Please don't save Buddy, he knows where he is and what he's doing better than you. Give Buddy a hug and a hot dog. Play with him all you want, and then let him go home and you do the same."

These days we've come to expect "lost Buddy" calls. They don't usually come until the second or third day. By the third day, the novelty of having a Buddy wears off on the potential dog-napper, but I'm not sure that is also true for Buddy.

As for Bud, I'll tell you what he doesn't like: the cold lonely pen the rangers use as his jailhouse in Cades Cove. That's where

Buddy in sun on
Little Bottoms Trail

he scribbled graffiti on the walls: *The Budro is here again*, like,
Kilroy was here.

Last Sunday, after church, I stopped for milk at the convenience store. The young lady at the cash register surprised me
and said, "I'm going camping at Abrams Creek and looking
forward to seeing Buddy, your dog." Yeah, everybody is. They
don't care about coming to see me!

Amanda Coada, who lives in Happy Valley, was photo-
graphing mushrooms two miles out from the campground one
morning. She was bent over just above a plant when she was
almost frightened to death by an animal's breath on her back.
She thought it was a bear! "Buddy's cold nose on my back nearly
gave me a heart attack," she said.

One day, the following email arrived out of the blue. It's from
a Mr. Hunter Foreman and his wife, Jan. They found out where
to reach Buddy's owners via the Foothills Land Conservancy.
With their permission, here is what they wrote:

Hey Bill,
Jan and I were doing our last maintenance hike of the season on
Little Bottoms Trail last Sunday, October 30. When we got to the
bottom of the steep hill where it turns left to follow Abrams Creek,
we met a man probably in his early 60's with short silvery hair,
and of course, accompanied by Buddy.

We talked with the guy for quite a while, and Buddy got bored and lay down in a sunny spot to take a nap. I've never seen him so worn out! You may know the man (we didn't ask his name, but he lives in Alcoa). He said he walks 3-4 times a week, and hikes with Buddy all the time. He said he always stops at the bathroom at the campground before hiking and leaves his pack outside. When he comes out, Buddy is waiting by his pack. He said that when he gets back to the campground, he opens the door to his van and Buddy hops right in. When he gets to the base of your driveway, he lets him out and he heads home.

He said, one time, a bunch of Boy Scouts were camping at Campsite #178, and Buddy left him to play with them. The next day he hiked up the same trail and, sure enough, met the Scouts coming out with Buddy leading the way. The man said he bought some good doggie treats some time ago to give Buddy while they were hiking, but Buddy wasn't interested at all. But, when he offered him a sugar wafer like he was eating, he loved it. We all agreed that Buddy is the coolest dog we've ever met! We're looking forward to seeing him when we start hiking again next spring . . . Hunter.

Note: Buddy's hiking friend is a retired marine named Dennie. Buddy likes to go with Dennie because on the way home Dennie drives The Bud Man all the way up the hill from the Park to the foot of our driveway. We usually know when Buddy has hiked with Dennie because he's always dragging back up the driveway. He's pooped and goes straight to his bed on our porch. Dennie likes to hike twelve miles or more on a trip. The last time I talked to him, he was off on a hiking trip to Michigan.

This other email came from a thru-hiker who first met The Bud Man nearly a year ago. Then, when she ran into him again a year later, she sent me this note:

Hi Bill,
Got a kick out of reading the story Elise forwarded me about Buddy! (Elise works with the Foothills Land Conservancy and knows Buddy, too.) *I wrote a little something for you about him and I hope you enjoy it! I'm currently in New Hampshire taking a day off from hiking the AT all the way to Maine.*

A Story for You about Buddy

When I decided I was going to attempt a thru hike of the Appalachian Trail, a 2184 mile footpath from Georgia to Maine, in the summer of 2011, I hadn't yet even spent one night alone in the woods. My longest trip ever had been two nights! I decided I needed to try it on my own and I needed to go to a site in the backcountry far enough off the road so that I would feel safe. I chose campsite 14 on the Hannah Mountain Trail since I hadn't yet hiked it and the roads near it were hard to access. I began my trip on a Tuesday morning from the Abrams Creek Campground unsure what to expect and I was more than a bit nervous to say the least. I had no idea what to expect over the next few hours!

I was the only person on the trail that morning, but when I came to the trail junction at campsite 16, I saw a group of four young men doing maintenance on the trails after an F-4 tornado had ripped through the Park last year. To my surprise there was another crew member with them, a dog! Dogs aren't allowed at all in the Smokies so I was shocked to see him. The even weirder thing was I recognized this dog as I'd seen him before on the Goldmine Trail further up the Cove. When I told the crew I recognized the dog, they told me they loved his company during the day, but now that a pretty woman had arrived, he would more than likely choose my company. Well, they weren't kidding because, as soon as I started up the trail, he followed.

The dog stayed right with me the entire time I walked to campsite 14, give, or take a few times he ran off after sniffing the ground. When I got to the campsite, I was ready for a break and my new friend lay at my feet. I decided to call my new friend Buddy, as he seemed like a good buddy to me. After discovering there was no water at the site, I decided to turn back around and go to campsite 16. I asked Buddy if he wanted to come and he did enthusiastically. He and I walked together back to the site. When I got there, he stayed with me until about 4:30 when I asked him if he was hungry. He had on a collar with an address, but no name. I told him to go home for dinner. He did and I didn't see him again that day.

My new buddy made me feel at ease on my first trip alone and it was comforting to have him there. I have a dog myself who loves to hike, so it was a great joy to have a companion. A few months later,

Buddy enjoying a scenic view

I hiked in this area again. As soon as I got out of my car, my buddy showed up, this time wearing a new collar and tag, this one with his name on it – Buddy! It made my entire day to see him again, and he hiked the entire 20 miles with me that day, going home when we got back to my car. Seems to me that this little guy, just like me, has a great love for the National Park and enjoys the trails just as much as we all do. This is a photo I took of my friend back in September 2011 on my first solo trip.

Jan Kelley – Aka Sprinkles (2012 thru hiker GA to ME)

The maintenance rangers at Abrams Creek Campground sometimes report that Buddy helps them clean and run the weed-eater. They like his company, particularly in the winter when it's so quiet. Yesterday, Ranger Marc drove up the driveway to our house. There was Buddy in the backseat, like he was coming home in a paddy wagon. He was looking out the window with those sad eyes.

"Busted again." It was written all over his face. I thanked Marc for bringing Buddy home.

"He's been paw-handling again."

"We'll try keeping him on the wire, I promise. Particularly over the weekend," I assured the ranger.

"Fine," he kindly replied. "I know he can't read, but there were a couple of people in the campground who didn't like an unleashed dog around their campsite."

"I understand," I said.

On various hikes through the campground up along Abrams Creek, Buddy and I have often seen a pair of otters playing in the creek. If you're quiet, you can watch otters play for a while before they skitter off. When Buddy saw I was hiding behind a big tree watching something, he finally saw them, too. He looked up at me and then began to whimper a little bit. It was his way of communicating with me, as if to say, "What are they? Well? Do you want me to go after them, eat them, scare them, what?"

No, Buddy. We're just lucky to see them.

A week or two ago, a youngish fellow, a camper on the Abrams Creek trail, told me that when he woke up one morning and looked out his pup tent, there was Buddy staring at him. He smiled telling me this. As we started walking along the trail

An otter playing

back toward the parking lot, this young man turned to me and thoughtfully asked, "Your dog isn't much of a bear dog, is he?"

That surprised me. I thought to myself, Old Bud sure keeps the bears off our porch. At night, he barks like a maniac when a bear comes around. He always lets us know when bears are nearby on his property. I've even seen him go after two bears at the same time. More than a few times, he'd bark and bark like crazy, pestering and even getting within ten feet of a bear. He can't scare a bear, but he'll sure bother it until finally it'll slowly amble off.

When I asked the fellow why he would ask the question, he explained: "I was walking up the trail with Buddy, your dog, when this big bear lumbered out onto the trail." Then the man laughed. "Ha! Your dog didn't bark or anything. He just took off running up the trail."

I thought about this for a while, studied on it, you might say. Running away from a bear, heading up the trail as the bear goes down it, is actually a pretty smart thing to do, isn't it? I mean, when you think about it.

Buddy posing on porch. A children's version of *Buddy: Dog of the Smoky Mountains* is available from Celtic Cat Publishing.

The Tomato War

When viewing pastoral Grainger County, Tennessee, one sees no hint of what is lurking behind the scenes—that it could exist at all, or that there even is such a thing as a tomato war.

Grainger County lies about forty-five miles north of Knoxville, up Rutledge Pike on Highway 11 West. It's a lush scenic drive through one of the most beautiful valleys in the world. It becomes a two-lane blacktop road as it meanders through rolling green farm country, nestled at the foot of Clinch Mountain. This alley of the Tennessee Valley between Clinch Mountain and the Great Smoky Mountains is a spectacularly beautiful place, always one of my favorites. It's not heaven; it's Grainger County.

It's a historic journey, too. Grainger County's Bean Station is a place of revolutionary origins, with Jackson, Sevier, and many other early historic figures traveling along this same path. This is the tomato capital of the world, with the best tomatoes anywhere. It's due partly to the rich, dark, fertile soil. But it's also due to the lifelong work of the county extension agent, Charlie Gavin, who has worked diligently for decades networking with the tomato growers, promoting and marketing the county's red wonders.

We've known Charlie since we began *The Heartland Series* in 1984 on WBIR-TV. He helped us on dozens of stories, and we've had a lot of fun. From Blaine to Bean Station and points in between, Charlie introduced us to many of the wonders and beauties of Grainger County. But his is a different tale, another story.

In 1988, we were invited to the Tomato Festival to participate in the first annual full-fledged tomato battle. What a day it was, too. Whew! It's the second most amazing thing I've ever had the privilege of doing in my life.

First off, what happens in a tomato war is pretty much what you'd expect. People throw tomatoes at you, and you throw them back. You use garbage-can lids, plywood sheets, or heavy cardboard for shields. There are two teams, ten against ten, with men and women on the same team. There are two fifty-gallon drums full of tomatoes, one per team, at each end of the field. There are three referees dressed in striped shirts. Everyone else wears shorts and white tee shirts so that, when you get hit, the referees can see where the tomato has splattered all over you.

You only learn this stuff – how to fight in a tomato war – through the experience of actually doing it. That's just the high price you have to pay. The actual war takes place on what looks like an eighty-yard football field, at least ours was. We played in the open field behind the old Grainger County High School. It was a single elimination tournament, part of the Tomato Festival that took place in the torpid heat of early August. By late afternoon, it was nearly one hundred degrees.

When someone gets hit by a tomato, the refs blow their whistles and everything stops. A determination is quickly made whether a "kill" has occurred. If so, the victim hurries off the field, disqualified. Then, the whistle blows and you commence fighting again while the eliminated person celebrates – they get to go home! This continues until a team is out of fighters, and I say "fighters" instead of "players" because that's what they're doing – fighting. This, of course, all happens very fast.

Thinking back on it now that I'm an old veteran of the tomato wars, it's not actually a game you're playing. This is for keeps. It really is a fight. That's why veterans refer to it as fighting in a tomato war. It's more like a brawl or a rumble than a game.

The only obstacle on the battlefield is a wagon. It's positioned smack in the middle of the field, and it quickly becomes clear, once the fighting starts, that whichever team controls the wagon has the advantage – they control the field. Not only is their fire-power increased, but they hold the only high ground and can throw downhill. This seems like a miniscule advantage, but trust me; you want to control the wagon, the hallowed ground of the battlefield.

We first heard of this tomato war business when we received a fairly anonymous one-page flyer. It looked innocent enough –

inviting "one and all to participate in a tomato war." Now, how can you pass that up? We were in. Hey, how many times do you get invited to a tomato war in your lifetime? Not many. . .if you're lucky.

So we rounded up nine other knuckleheads who wanted to spend a hot Saturday in August fighting in a tomato war. The only prerequisite was that you needed to be able to throw a fastball. And, though we didn't know it then, you also needed to enjoy receiving pain and inflicting it on others. Teams came from other Knoxville TV stations, ITT and Intel Corporation, U.T. Library, and many others. There were nearly twenty-five teams in all. As far as I know, few of us had ever done this before. We just didn't know any better. We were all bamboozled.

This being the first year, the good folks in Grainger County were very excited about hosting the event and putting their best foot forward, so the tomato growers sent their very best fruit. But here was the problem: they didn't send their mushy, soft, old, and gooey tomatoes, which would have been fine. Instead, they donated their very best one- and two-pounders; their beautiful, big, red, round, rock-hard tomatoes.

You see, tomatoes are usually picked when they're hard. They ripen and soften in transit or on store shelves. By the time they get to the buyer, they're soft. Not the ones we used that day. The tomatoes we used were heavy and hard as bricks. It was like throwing ice balls, or big rocks. The only way to protect yourself was to go home.

The problem was that a one-pound tomato traveling at seventy or eighty miles-per-hour could rip a shield right out of your hand, bust your glasses, and even dislocate a vertebra or two. These are actual injuries that happened. WVLT-TV, Channel 8 weekend anchor Allen Williams caught one right between the eyes. It was a fastball thrown by our very own Julie Taylor. He showed up on the air the next week with a black eye. All's fair in the tomato wars!

I'm convinced one Grainger County factory team had some semi-pro baseball players. One guy was obviously a pitcher for somebody like the Yankees, no doubt, or I'm a monkey's uncle. This guy looked like a bounty hunter. He didn't even carry a shield. His team kept him surrounded with two or three defend-

Pitcher firing in 2012 Tomato Wars

ers, using their shields to guard him at all times. All this guy did was throw tomatoes, and he could hum them, too. To beat this team, we had to eliminate him as their offensive weapon. This guy was one dangerous threat to life and limb.

Thinking back on it after all these years, I still wonder how I got sucked into this thing. It sounded simple enough at the time. We didn't know we were going to battle five times and fight all day to the death. I still wake up at night in a cold sweat, my eyes peeled, my heart pumping, and my head on a swivel. I should get treatment. It's been almost fifteen years since that horrible day. I had played football – that was a rugged game. But this was much tougher than football. This was like a rock fight. Each match was like a knife fight in a ditch. It was officially sanctioned murder; warriors were getting blasted by the dozens out there!

It was just like throwing bricks all day. My arm felt like a limp piece of rope after three fights. That's how bad it hurt from throwing hard, heavy tomatoes one right after another. My arm ached so much after our quarter-final bout, I couldn't lift it. We were all just bloody, mushy spaghetti sauce mixtures out there.

The only reason we survived to fight another match, then another and another, was because of our shields. We had the best shields, no doubt about it. It was pure luck, for before the fight, we didn't know how critically important our choice of shield material would be.

A week prior to the battle, Doyle Dixon, our head carpenter at the station (and our *only* carpenter) happened to have some three-quarter-inch, double-corrugated cardboard lying around in his basement. We didn't even know they made boxes this strong. It was light, too. With this material, Doyle saved our bacon. It was like armor. Boy, we were lucky.

But we still had to secure the shields to our arms somehow. So we tied short pieces of scrap rope with a peg on each end, securing it through the cardboard. It served us well. The only problem was it burned all the hair and half the skin off our forearms. But, it protected our head and groin areas. That's what counted.

Those shields worked great. When hit, they gave. They would bend a little, cushioning the blow. And they were light enough so at the last second you could whip your shield around to block the flying rocks coming at you. Opposing fighters were trying to take your head off, and did, too, occasionally. There were bloody heads rolling around everywhere. It was awful! (Okay, I'm exaggerating, but only a little bit.)

My son Jack, Julie, and I volunteered to paint our company's logo on the shields. Instead of "Straight from the Heart," we painted a fierce-looking, bloody-red tomato face artistically crafted into a skull-and-crossbones motif. It looked cool, bizarre, and mean; Jolly Roger tomato faces in the station's colors, of course. We painted all ten of our teams' shields with these leering faces, complete with blood dripping from the corners of their mouths. Those shields spread fear and terror in the hearts of our opponents. It gave us the winning edge we needed. (See Plate 17.)

On the other side of the field, the shield of choice, a garbage-can lid, just didn't hold up — be it corrugated metal, tin, or even heavy plastic. These types of shields didn't last two battles, and neither did the people using them. Doomed, they were. It was only a matter of time before their fighters were destroyed. The reason is this: an eighty-mile-per-hour, one-pound, flying tomato can rip a garbage can lid right out of your hand. This leaves defenders naked, holding a handle and nothing else. I saw it happen again and again. It leaves them standing there, with goofy, quizzical looks on their faces, whistling in the wind.

Only teams that put thought, time, and planning into their choice of shield material and construction had any chance of surviving and advancing. Other successful shields, for instance, included some made from three-quarter-inch plywood. These shields were strong, but too heavy to maneuver. Quarter-inch plywood worked much better. Many in this style were attractively decorated and quite impressive.

The day of the tomato war started out like any other hot summer day. Arriving at the big field behind old Rutledge High School at 9 a.m., we loosened up by doing some exercises. But even that early, it was way too hot for much of that nonsense. Then, the gentle breeze mysteriously quit blowing and died out completely. We took that as a bad omen.

Everything was wet from the early morning dew. The field was chalked up like before a ball game: outlined, complete with multi-colored banners surrounding the field. It was quite impressive, but ominous somehow.

Again, you have to understand—nobody had ever seen a tomato fight before or at least witnessed one on such a massive scale and lived to tell about it. No team, none of the athletes—and I use this term loosely—had ever even seen a battle, much less fought in one. We didn't know the first thing about what was going on, what to do, or how to do it. We were all just fodder out there. We aimed to throw 'maters and try not to get pummeled. That's all we knew about it.

There were hundreds, perhaps even thousands of people already there, come to watch this gruesome spectacle. We were like Roman gladiators, and this was the arena. I guess the audience didn't have anything better to do. They didn't know it, but they were about to watch a real Romanesque blood bath. Come to think of it, that's probably why they came, what they expected to see, and why they had such a good time.

Well, they got their money's worth—monumental slaughter, an entire day's worth of it; blood and carnage everywhere. A thousand people participated. Well, not quite a thousand. More like two-hundred-fifty idiots—I mean "athletes." But, that's not including subs, medical support, and ambulance personnel.

We learned from the experience of watching the other poor fools get clobbered. "Keep your head down, shield up, and move fast in groups." If you didn't pick up these basic techniques and instructions, you went home with a busted lip, hurt pride, or worse. As the day progressed, going home, throwing in your shield (and burning it), became the more attractive alternative.

We were grasping at straws. Take something as simple as carrying the tomatoes, for instance. Nobody knew to bring a little bag. We found we needed something to carry our tomatoes in, but we had to figure out what. We had to adapt, learn this stuff while ducking and dodging tracers. The tomato drums were stationary, immovable. Without some way to carry your ammo on your person, you were stuck standing by the drums. It made you stationary, as in a stationary target. No, you didn't want that. Without a baggie, it was difficult to carry even three or four 'maters as you moved up, down, and around the field looking for somebody to whack.

The problem, therefore, was how to carry your tomatoes, hold your shield, and keep your throwing arm free at the same time. Fighters grabbed popcorn bags from people in the stands. We used convenience-store baggies, extra shirts, pockets, anything we could find that would carry a tomato.

If you stuffed tomatoes in your pockets, you couldn't get them out fast enough, and you also couldn't carry enough like that. Besides, a tomato in your pocket will explode when it gets hit. That's no good; it looks too much like you've wet your pants. We eventually found out that the best method was to carry a baggie behind your shield and keep your throwing arm free.

As the day got hotter, so did the battles. I'll always remember one fight in particular. The factory team had the poor U.T. Library team down to nine or eight against two. We watched as the bounty hunters surrounded and were about to destroy the librarians. It was obviously turning into a massacre. Many people turned away. They just couldn't watch it.

We thought, "This could get ugly." But it was already ugly! And then all at once, something amazing happened. The factory fighters all knelt down on one knee as they surrounded the last two librarians. Then, they raised one arm in the air with a tomato in hand. "What are they doing?" someone yelled. Then, it dawned on us. They were honoring them. It was the Klingon war salute.

The Star Trek gesture brought a big lump to the throats of all those who witnessed it before it brought a lump to the heads of the librarians from incoming 'maters. It was certainly one of the more noble gestures witnessed. They were recognizing the gallant effort and courage of the brave librarians, even though they were the enemy and were getting crushed.

It brought to mind certain Blackfoot and other Native American traditions, where a tribe's strength is measured by the strength of its enemy; the fiercer the enemy, the braver the tribe. If that's true, the librarians might actually be a lot braver and stronger than they appeared, but I doubt it. We learned this stuff from *Star Fleet* and watching *Jeremiah Johnson*.

My son Jack brought his friend, Matt Ryan, from down the street to bolster our play. They mistakenly thought they would have fun. Ha, fun, alright! Mere survival is all we wanted. We had Julie, the killer princess, on our team. Ruth, Joe Cable, Jarrell, and others fought well and bravely. But, by the fourth fight of the day, most of the sane people had either gone home or to the hospital, and we didn't have enough people left to form a team. Yikes!

Some of us stayed all day—mostly because we couldn't get a ride home. Jack and Matt, being sixteen, could have fought all day and all night, too. Julie was itching and ready to go. She was like our captain. I personally couldn't lift my arm at all for the final two matches. I just wasn't any good at the end, but at least I was out there. We had no combat reserves.

The young and crazy still had life in them, but that's all. In those two final matches, I have to admit we did pick up what might be construed as two ringers. We're not proud of it, but it was necessary. It took a hardened heart and steel reserve, and a head with no brains, to stay out there all day. I can't blame anyone for heading home and straight to the hot tub.

We held no animosity. By three p.m., some of our Channel 10 teammates, after fighting valiantly all day, had skipped town, va-

There's no cover
in a Tomato fight

Boy, that was close

moosed. They'd skedaddled, gone to soak their battered bones and psyches. They'd done enough. So, we added Bunky. . .or Bucky. I can't remember his last name or even his first name. I just know he wore a Viking helmet with two big horns protruding from either side. He and another gunslinger played for our team in the last two battles, the semi-finals, and the finals.

We needed them, or we would have had to forfeit those fights. Besides, they made us a better team. Bucky's wife photographed every match all day using a video camcorder. This was a bonus. She recorded all Bucky's matches, exploits, and various killings and had a ball doing it. They were a cute couple.

Bucky was built like a catcher and weighed about two-hundred-twenty-five pounds. With his horns and Viking helmet he was frightening—a good guy to have on your side no matter

Two-fisted fighter

what you had to pay him. Adding him and the other hired gun broke our opponents' spirits. It wrecked their mental capabilities for the match; and, as it turned out later, their ability to sire any more children.

No, it certainly didn't hurt us to have Bucky on our team. His screaming fastball hit more than a few opponents between their shoulder blades about the L-3 vertebrae and paralyzed two of them—just temporarily, though. By supper time, after a full day in 100-degree heat, we were all bear caught, like in *Cool Hand Luke*. Only two teams remained standing, although wobbly on their feet—us and our ringers, and the factory team.

This was the finals for all the marbles. Everything was on the line. If we could take out their pro pitcher, we had a chance. That was the plan, our strategy from the get-go. We concentrated all our firepower on his defenses, managing to wipe out his shield-carrying entourage. First, we took out his protectors. Then, we cleaned his clock. The whistle blew and he was out cold, sort of. He'd caught one upside the head. I don't know who threw it. Probably it was Julie—a real Amazon warrior princess. She had taken out Allen Williams earlier. I bet he's still picking little pieces of tomato-bisque out of his left eye. We were lucky she fought for us.

Amidst cries of pain and screams of delirium and relief, we celebrated our greatest victory, our grandest achievement—other than sneaking out that night on Missionary Ridge, but that's another story. Immediately, smack in the middle of our victory celebration, an old van pulled up and screeched to a halt. It was the jubilant Viking, Bucky. He stuck his head out the side door with tomato juice still dripping from his helmet and motioned for us all to pile in. So, we grabbed our trophies and medals and, without thinking, climbed aboard. With Mrs. Bucky driving, we screamed out of there, careening in the air,

If you're here, you're suspect

bouncing hard when we landed, and with no idea where we were going, or why.

Out on the road, Mrs. Bucky was driving more cautiously. After traveling a few miles we ended up somewhere in a forest near a big stream. We could never have found the place ourselves in a hundred years. It looked like a lagoon in the middle of the forest. Our vehicle drove right up almost into the big creek. High above, nearly fifteen feet up, was a giant pipe, gushing cool water out over our heads. It was like a big shower, a place where local folks brought their trucks to fill them up and, later, water their tobacco fields.

It was a spectacularly beautiful place. Here, as the cool water bathed over us, together we celebrated our victory. We were now all veterans of the tomato wars. It felt so refreshing, as the water ran over our bruised and sunburned bodies and washed away the spaghetti sauce, seeds, and smashed tomatoes from ears, hair, and clothes. We even lay down in the stream. We celebrated together, this victorious team. We'd won! It meant quite a lot. Mostly, it meant we'd never have to do this again.

We rushed back to the studio with the video Bucky's wife recorded, and Gene Patterson managed to get it on the six-o'clock news. It didn't mean much unless you were part of that winning team. Then, it meant everything in the world. A year later, in spite of great trepidation, in a moment of weakness we reluctantly agreed to defend our title in the second annual Grainger County Tomato War.

You can't believe how relieved we were when returning to the battleground the following year we discovered only one other team had signed up. Everyone else knew better. Ha! I guess everybody wised up. Either that, or after only a year, people's injuries hadn't healed completely. We were elated. I think we cried. We dispatched our competition quickly, won a baseball cap, got out of there, and went home to count our blessings.

We didn't land in Normandy or fight at the Battle of the Bulge or in the Pacific. But, a tomato fight is something I'm glad to have done once, actually twice, which was enough for me, thank you. I wouldn't trade the experience for almost anything in the world. But, I don't ever want to do it again. No sir, I don't ever want to fight in another tomato war as long as I live.

Bill's Little Stories

One day in Grainger County, the county extension agent, Charlie Gavin, stopped by to see John Fugate on his pig farm.

He found John out in the orchard under the apple tree. The hogs had eaten all the apples on the ground, so John was picking up a pig and lifting it up so it could snag an apple off a limb. He did this one right after the other – holding the pig so it could eat a nice juicy apple.

"Hey John," Charlie said. "Boy, isn't that a lot of work picking pigs up like that just so they can eat an apple? Doesn't that take a lot of time?"

John looked at Charlie and without a pause replied, "What's time to a pig?"

Over Home in Hancock County

As a former Hancock County administrator for thirty-two years, Scotty Collins is a respected leader and city father in Sneedville, Tennessee. We first met twenty-five years ago when he was the circuit court clerk there, and we have been friends ever since. I consider Mr. Collins a great friend.

Scotty was always helpful to *The Heartland Series* on our Hancock County stories. Without Scotty's help, we would never have met Jep Mackey and Randy Trent, first heard about Mahalia Mullins, the great old moonshiner, or many other special people and stories. Scotty is a gentleman of the Melungeon persuasion, the dark-skinned, blue-eyed people who were here when John Sevier first entered this county, and he explained the origins of his people to us.

From Scotty Collins and the work of writer/historian Dr. Brent Kennedy, whose books address the Melungeon people's origins; we learned that they are direct descendants of the Portuguese and Moroccan explorers that first came with Juan Pardo's Spanish expedition in the 16th century. They stayed and intermingled with the Native Americans and other peoples. Their descendants were collectively called Melungeons.

Newman's Ridge, in Hancock County, is supposedly the place where the Melungeons originated. It is a mountain, but a community, as well. It's a remote, tough, hard-scrabble, big, long, mountain where those blue-eyed, olive-skinned folks retreated to. In Sneedville, you meet a lot of people with names like Goins, Collins, and Mullins. These are Melungeon names. This is where the Varde Collins clan sprang from, or retreated to, whichever way you look at it.

As helpful as he was to *The Heartland Series*, Scotty's most important job has always been to help the people in Hancock County. It's a poor county with 1,500 people in Sneedville and

Cecile Turner by clean, pure headwaters of the Clinch River

around 6,000 residents in the county. The average household income is about $12,000 a year. The only other community in Hancock County is Kyle's Ford. Sneedville is not really a city, and Kyle's Ford is even smaller, with a few cabins, a building or two, and a restaurant that serves fabulous food.

Scotty is a banker now and says he has about a dozen folks to whom he lends money occasionally to help them make ends meet. They repay him when they can, and he keeps records, but it's not officially official, if you know what I mean. It's more like the way things were done in small towns fifty to a hundred years ago. A few years ago, I was Grand Marshall of the annual Christmas parade. While Scotty and I visited outside the Sneedville County Courthouse before the parade, a fellow resident came by, thanked Scotty quietly, and slipped him forty dollars that he'd borrowed twenty at a time on two different occasions.

An interesting thing about Sneedville is everyone refers to it as "over home." If you are from Sneedville and leave—say to work in Morristown—and you talk about Sneedville, that's what you call it: over home. Everybody does. For example, someone asks, "Where you going?" Everybody knows what you mean when you respond, "over home." It's the only place I've ever heard referred to that way. That's Sneedville, in Hancock County.

You have to want to come to Sneedville. It's almost three hours from Knoxville, tucked deep into the far dark ridges and mountains. It's forty miles to Kingsport, a stone's throw to Virginia, and about thirty miles to Mooresburg and Tazewell. Hancock County and Sneedville are not places people just pass through. They are the destination. It's the "far land," over the ridges and the mountains. We usually get there by heading up Highway 11 West past Blaine in Grainger County, through Rogersville. Then, after traveling about twenty-five miles on state road 31, you go another twenty-five miles and climb a 2,500- to 3,000-foot mountain before going down the other side. You'll cross War Creek and come to the Clinch River. Go upstream, cross the bridge and you're over home.

Once, *Heartland* videographer Doug Mills and I were shooting footage of beautiful Hancock County for a spring story. While standing on the old War Creek Bridge, we looked down into the crystal-clear water below. It was full of fat, ten-inch fish. They were schooling around when suddenly something attacked. Boom! With knife-like precision, out from the weeds, we couldn't see where, a snake struck. It looked like someone had thrown a spear and gaffed a big fish and the fish was stuck on the end of a stick. But it was actually a snake that had attacked the fish and wouldn't let go. The fish was so big that the seven-foot snake was thrashing around in the water and weeds. The fish was too big to give up, and the snake couldn't swallow it, but wouldn't let go. It was a stand-off, a fierce struggle that continued until we lost sight of it in the high grass along the stream bank.

We recorded it. I've never forgotten this little thirty-second image. It was like a morality play, serving as a microcosm of the rugged nature of Hancock County: pastoral, beautiful, yet with a touch of danger; a complex, but glorious struggle; life on the edge, maybe. It's a good place, but it's a tough place. The people there have always been hard-working folks, and they always settle things amongst themselves.

There are stories of people getting shot, sometimes by the sheriff, and of multiple meth labs and meth cases in recent years—hard living and hard times. There's twenty-percent unemployment. It's a place where ten or twenty years ago, when we first visited, a man might have four tobacco fields and har-

The Knoxu[...]

Independe[...]

122ND YEAR

KNOX[...]

scattered showers and thundershowers. High today
[...]. Low tonight [...]. High yesterday 79. Low this
morning [...].
NORTH CAROLINA: Partly cloudy. Scattered
thundershowers. High around 80.
VIRGINIA: Warm with afternoon showers. High
in 70s.
KENTUCKY: Cloudy. Warm. Showers. High 60-70.
(Weather Details on Page 143)

Six Charged With Murde[...]
Riddled In Sneedville Gu[...]

★ ★ ★ ★ ★ ★ ★ ★ ★ ★ ★ ★ ★ ★ ★

France Prepares For W[...]

Attack By Air Foreseen

PARIS, Monday, April
24 (P) — President Charles
de Gaulle today placed
France virtually on a war
footing to combat a military
insurrection in Algeria —
and a possible parachutist
attack on France.

Shortly after De Gaulle invoked
almost absolute powers, under
the constitution, to deal with the
insurrectionists, Minister Michel
Debre went on the air to warn
the population that a parachute
attack from Algeria could be expected at any moment.

There were reports early today
that paratroops already had taken
off from airfields in Algeria.

Cultural Affairs Minister Andre
Malraux was quoted as saying a
paratroop landing could be attempted in the next three hours.

Fighter planes were ordered to
shoot down any unauthorized air-
craft in French skies.

All landing fields in the Paris
area were ordered to be made un-
usable by 2 a. m. Trucks, cars
and other obstacles were placed
on runways.

TROOPS ALERTED

Security troops throughout the
nation were ordered to be in
readiness. In Paris an extra 10,000
specially trained riot and security
troopers were called out to join
an already strong force stationed
at vital points.

The atmosphere in the capital

Staff photos by Tom Greene J[...]

FEUD TRAGEDY—Mrs. Georgia Morris (left) mourns as she displays her
dead husband's symbols of heroism in two wars. The husband, Deputy Alex G.
Morris, of Sneedville, died with a bullet in his back last night as a month-
long grudge between two Hancock County law enforcement officers erupted in
gunplay. Deputy Morris received five Purple Heart medals for wounds suffered
in six major campaigns of World War II and the Korean Conflict. At right, officers question suspects in the triple-slayings in a lineup at the Sneedville Jail.
From left to right, are Tennessee Bureau of Identification Agent J. H. Bauer,
State Trooper Sterling Trent, George Myers, James Horton, Earl Myers, Carl
Myers and E. A. Myers, and Deputy Elwood Hurd, who escaped the gunfight.
The Myerses and Horton are charged with murder. Note Horton's swollen eyes,
the result of a shot from Deputy Hurd's tear gas pistol. (More Pictures on
Page 8.)

...the Journal   City Edition

...ned And Operated

MONDAY, APRIL 24, 1961   20 Pages : : Two Sections   PRICE 5 CENTS

r As Three Killed, Sheriff
nfight Ignited By Grudge

*   *   *   *   *   *   *   *   *   *

r Following Insurrection

State Troopers Ride In Tense Aftermath Of Officer Slayings

By BILL BOLUS
Journal Reporter

SNEEDVILLE, April 23—Six persons were charged today with first degree murder in the aftermath of a gunbattle which left two sheriff's deputies and a constable dead, and Hancock County Sheriff Verlin Maxey near death.

Dead are:

Constable C. B. Oaks, 31.
Deputy Sheriff Alex Morris, 48.
Deputy Sheriff A. J. (Lon) Tyler, 50.

Charged are:

Madison Oaks, father of Constable Oaks, released under $10,000 bond.
E. A. Myers, 31, who is married to Constable Oak's sister.
Earl Myers, 34, Franklin, Ohio.
Carl Myers, 38, Miamisburg, Ohio.
George Myers, 57, Thorn Hill.
James Allen Horton, 19, nephew of Constable Oaks.
George Myers is the father of E. A., Earl and Carl Myers.

The bloody battle took place at 10:45 p. m. yesterday at the home of Matt Oaks, long time Hancock County farmer, and cast a pall of tragedy over this small mountain town.

The gunbattle, erupting after a month-long feud between Sheriff Maxey and Constable Oaks, according to investigators, lasted only a couple of minutes.

But in that time Constable Oaks was cut down with a bullet dead center in his chest, the two deputies suffered fatal wounds in the back and Sheriff Maxey was shot in the abdomen and twice in the left arm.

SHOOTINGS APPEARED PLANNED

Investigators said the shootings appeared to have been planned and that the sheriff and his men walked into an ambush at the Oaks residence.

Horton today was still suffering the effects of tear gas fired at him during the melee by Deputy Elwood Hurd, who lived to tell of the battle though himself beaten and stomped.

Sheriff Maxey was reported in surgery at Baptist Hospital in Knoxville, struggling to survive the three bullet wounds and a merciless ...ing ...stomping he suffered after being shot.

Link Green epitomized tough Sneedville characters

vest four acres yearly to make a living. At $2,000 an acre, that's $8,000 for year-round work—hard work, which tobacco farming has always been. Tobacco is gone now and, with it, a lot of people's pride and the ability to make good Christmas money. Scotty says good marijuana plants would bring $1,500 apiece. So, four plants would equal growing and harvesting about three acres of tobacco.

I remember Mark Twain writing about the "Southerner's penchant for violence." But, he was referring to Knoxville after the famous Thomas Mabry shootout between a banker and a lawyer and their seconds and thirds. When the smoke cleared that day, seven or eight lay dead. It happened right there on Gay Street in downtown Knoxville.

In describing Hancock County, I'd have to say that it isn't quite as mean as some other places, although some particular people might be. But, according to the many good folks we talked to recently, it's just a way of life. The sheriff is all the time coming across someone killed from some dispute. Oftentimes, it's over a woman. But, it could be over almost anything. "Good a people as you'll find anywhere, but they'll just kill you," is the way they put it. Disagreements happen everywhere, but in Hancock County they often lead to shootouts.

"People here have always taken care of themselves," says Linda Burke's husband, Jerry. "They'll just shoot ya. As good a people as you'll find anywhere, but just don't disagree with them or get into a dispute. They'll kill you. My great, great, grandfather was like that. Uncle Link, they called him. His name was Lincoln Green."

Scotty related to us one personal example. Scotty said his father and the Hancock County sheriff got into it in the street right in front of the Courthouse where I was standing for the annual Christmas parade. I spoke to a nice crowd right where Scotty's father got shot and where Scotty's father almost killed the sheriff

Mountaineer, Accused in Shooting, Keeps on Dress

Only Changes for Another Brought to Him in Hancock County Jail.

By ISAAC GIVENS
News-Sentinel Correspondent

SNEEDVILLE, Tenn., Nov. 26.— White - whiskered Lincoln Green still wears a dress in Hancock County jail, just as he did back in the hills.

The keen-eyed mountaineer was recently held to court on a charge of shooting his daughter, Myrtle, and her son-in-law, Charley Bailey, at Short Mountain. His bond was set at $1000 on that charge

Wearing his dress, 76-year-old Lincoln Green is shown on the steps of the Hancock County court house at Sneedville. At his side is George A. Williams, attorney of near Treadway, Tenn.

Mountaineer, accused in shooting, keeps on dress. —Sharon Cantwell

But he wasn't above escaping in a dress!

who had shot him. According to the story, both men had been drinking—which, by the way, is how many stories of this type begin. For some reason, the sheriff just took out his pistol and took a shot at Scotty's father. The sheriff missed him, but the sound of the bullet striking the ground sure attracted Scotty's father's attention, and he turned and looked up. He saw the sheriff shoot again. This time, his aim was better, and he hit Scotty's father in the shoulder.

Well, according to Scotty, and this must have been somewhat painful and difficult for him to recall, Mr. Collins reached up and grabbed the sheriff's gun hand at his wrist, holding his shooting arm up in the air with the gun still in it, so he couldn't get off another shot. But, the sheriff spun around, and Scotty's father took out his pocket-knife. He quickly opened it with one hand, so as not to release the grip on the sheriff's arm, stuck the short blade

Downtown
Sneedville, 1966

Coy Collins lived to be
95 years young

in the middle of the sheriff's butt, and jerked it up with a mighty slash.

"My father went away to Brushy Mountain Penitentiary for eighteen months, where he worried about what would happen if he saw the sheriff again when he got out. Meanwhile the sheriff spent months in the hospital. Of course, eventually they did meet again. One day my father was in town, coming up the street in front of the courthouse. The sheriff was up ahead in the street and saw my father. It was the first time he'd seen him since their confrontation. They walked slowly toward each other. When they got close, they both stuck out their hands and shook hands."

As Scotty was telling me this, he stuck out his hand to mimic it, and then he said that both men cried. "They cried and put their arms around each other."

It is quite a story, a fitting example of the unique people and place that is Sneedville and Hancock County. "They'll just shoot ya, but usually not without a cause . . . unless they've been drinking. People just always take care of their differences and settle things themselves. It's just the way it's always been around here."

It's the end of the journey. People don't much come through here. You have to be headed here. This is a destination, the end of the line. It's over home.

Mountain Remedies

Cures and Potions from Cocke County

Cures and potions are as peculiar to the mountain people as their language. We were fortunate to meet Doc Barton, Illa Hatter, and many others over the years and hear stories and tales about herbs, healings, and potions.

The list below was collected by the students from the folklore class at Cosby High School in Cocke County in 1974. It was first published by the *Newport Plain Talk* newspaper on October 15, 1986, and is used with their permission.

1. For coughs: take mullen plants, place them in a white cloth, and boil. Mix with rock candy, whiskey, and brown sugar.

2. To treat a baby's cold: take an onion and core it. Place sulfur in the middle and cover with a dry rag. Place it in hot ashes and cover. Let it cook about one hour. Remove onion from rags and strain through a clean rag into a cup or bottle. Feed liquid to the baby.

3. To cure sores: mix pure lard and sulfur to create a salve. Rub on sore.

4. To treat a fever blister: put ear wax on it.

5. Snuff placed on stings draws out the pain.

6. For a cold: mix whiskey, rock candy, and honey.

7. To rid a baby from worms: rub turpentine on the child's navel and throat.

8. To treat poison ivy: take some cedar and burn it. While the cedar is burning, hold the afflicted area over the smoke.

9. Another cough remedy is a mixture of brown sugar and vinegar. Drink as needed.

10. To induce vomiting: drink a mixture of mustard and water.

11. For sprains, soak a piece of brown paper in vinegar and wrap around the injured area.

12. Cigarette smoke blown into an ear will cure the earache.

13. For boils ("risins"): place a piece of fat meat on the sore.

14. To cure pinkeye: mash a raw potato and wrap in a cloth. Place on the eye.

15. To cure hiccoughs: eat one teaspoon of dry sugar.

16. To cure warts: sell them, but don't spend the money.

17. Alum and honey mixed together and swabbed in the mouth will cure the thrash.

18. Mayonnaise will take away sunburn pain.

19. To ensure an easy delivery: hang a pair of pants over the bed.

20. Eat ashes for a headache.

21. To cure warts: tie a thread around them, create a knot, and then bury the string under the eaves of the house.

22. Urine poured on athlete's foot will cure it.

23. Another wart removal method calls for one to count the number of warts and bury the same number of chicken bones under a beech tree. Turn and never go back to that place.

24. To stop bleeding: sprinkle powdered rice on lint and apply to the wound.

25. Another method to stop bleeding is to place a handful of flour over the cut.

26. Cobwebs bound on a wound will stop the bleeding.

27. Hazeline applied to cuts also stops bleeding.

28. To cure the itch, boil pole roots and then take a bath in the same water.

29. In the winter, melt snow and store until warm weather. This water placed on sunburns draws out the pain.

30. Horse mint and sugar boiled into tea cures an upset stomach.

31. Correctly repeating Ezekiel 16:6 will stop bleeding.

32. Scrapings from a cow's horn mixed into tea are a cure for fever.

33. Jerusalem oats mixed with molasses or honey are good for worms.

34. Chew burdock roots to soothe a sore mouth.

35. Tea made from boiled poke roots helps cure rheumatism.

36. Coal oil is good for a sore throat.

37. Beef tallow is good for chest cold and/or chapped hands.

38. Oil drained on a chin is good for an earache.

39. Cream, butter, or motor oil soothes sunburn pain.

40. Turpentine is good for snake bites, cuts, or sores.

41. Linseed oil is good for burns.

42. To stop a toothache: try turpentine or camphor.

43. Mix whiskey and sugar together and rub on the skin to cure measles.

44. To unclog sinuses: suck warm saltwater up the nose, and then spit out.

45. To prevent toothaches: carry a hog's tooth.

46. Boiled catnip and sugar given to babies cures them of hives.

47. Boil mint and drink it to stop diarrhea.

48. Scraped bark, placed in a cloth, draws pus out of a boil.

49. For a mashed finger: bore a hole in the fingernail to release the blood.

50. For a black eye: place a piece of fat meat on the injured area.

51. For a toothache: try either parched or browned soda.

52. If he sticks a nail in his foot, he should soak his foot in hot salt water to draw the soreness out. Then, place turpentine on the wound.

53. Larkspur lotion rids one of lice.

54. Ginger and boneset tea will help cure the gripe.

55. Fry onions and make a poultice. This placed on the chest cures the croup.

56. Burdock roots hung around baby's neck helps it teethe.

57. Heated whiskey and lemon juice cures the stomachache.
58. Drink about two ounces of boiled red alder for yellow jaundice.
59. Boil yellow roots, then, rinse out mouth to cure mouth sores.
60. Take white horse mint of boneset and hang it up and let it cure out. This boiled into tea helps cure colds.
61. Boiled burdock roots rid one of eczema.
62. Boil May apples and Jerusalem oak into tea as a cure for worms.
63. Boiled Balm-of-Gilead bulbs made into a salve eases pain from burns.
64. Boil burdock roots into tea. Sip three times a day for boils.
65. Rub castor oil on seed warts every night before retiring. The warts should disappear in a few days.
66. To stop a nose bleed, place a piece of rolled-up brown paper between the victim's upper lip and gum.
67. To stop bleeding from a cut, place a piece of hornet's nest over the wound.
68. Yellow root tea builds up the blood.
69. Ground ivy tea cures babies from hives.
70. Cherry bark, rock candy, and whiskey cure asthma.
71. Wilted beech tree leaves draw out boils.
72. Ground hog oil rubbed on the chest cures the croup.
73. Sheep dung boiled into tea will make measles break out.
74. Chew ginseng (sang) roots to cure stomach trouble.
75. Boil peach tree leaves into tea for a cold remedy.
76. Asafetida worn around the neck wards off diseases.
77. Cream taken off sweet milk heals sunburn.
78. Butter and salt eases the itching from chigger bites.
79. To remove warts: cut an "X" on the wart. Take a kernel of corn and drop the blood from the wart into the corn. Feed the corn to a chicken and the wart will go away.

80. Another wart removal remedy calls for one to take an old dish rag, rub it across the wart, then throw the dish rag into a mud hole. Leave and never look back.

81. Some men, often supposed to be the seventh son of a seventh son, have the ability to cure babies of thrash. To do so, the man takes the child to the barn, rubs a corn cob in their mouth while quoting a verse from the bible. Others blow their breath into the child's mouth.

82. Oatmeal and buttermilk made into paste removes pimples.

83. Tie a dirty sock around the neck to cure a sore throat.

84. To remove fuzz on a woman's face, rub a lemon over it.

85. Another wart removal cure calls for taking three yellow corn kernels and putting on a sarong. Seesaw them over the wart and feed them to a black chicken.

86. A sure-fired method of wart removal calls for rubbing beans on the warts, then tying the beans in a paper bag and leaving them at the forks of the road. Don't look back. The person who picks up the bag will get the warts.

87. Drink red sassafras tea in the springtime to thin your blood.

88. To cure a toothache: bore a hole in a dogwood tree. Make your gums bleed on cotton. Stuff cotton in the hole in your tooth; then put cotton in the hole in the tree.

89. Mullen baths stop swelling in feet and legs. They're also good for heart dropsy.

90. Cook barefoot root, add lard and salt to make a salve for rheumatism.

91. Tea from May apple roots relieves constipation.

92. Cherry root tea improves the appetite.

93. For "female troubles," drink tea made from tansy, red shank, or hazel roots.

94. Tea from ginseng roots cures the stomachache.

95. Tea boiled from dogwood bark cures poison ivy.
96. For snakebites to animals: take rattlesnake weed, beat it, and place in sweet milk. Give to bitten animal.
97. To cure colic in cows and horses: give them linseed oil to drink.
98. Raw potatoes placed on styes cures them.
99. To cure the itch: grease yourself with sulfur and lard for nine days. Do not bathe or change clothes.

Tea Remedies

100. Dandelion tea is good for the blood.
101. Ginger tea is good for the stomach.
102. Peppermint tea cures the colic.
103. Yellow dock and burdock tea cleans the blood and helps the liver
104. Licorice relieves common colds and sore throats.
105. Sage tea is good for the liver and blood.
106. Wintergreen tea helps wounds, sores, kidneys, and bladder.
107. Horsetail grass tea is good for bladder ailments.
108. Tea from juniper berries cures poor memory.
109. Kidney liver leaf tea helps cure ailments of the stomach, liver, and kidneys.
110. For whooping cough: take holly berries and chestnut leaves and boil them together. Mix with honey and drink.
111. For croup: take mutton tallow; mix with coal oil and turpentine. Put this mixture in a woolen cloth and put it on the patient's chest.

The D.F.O. File

Glenn Cardwell, the mayor of Pittman Center, our old friend from the Great Smoky Mountains National Park, had invited me to speak to the Sevier County Historical Society — to "sing for my supper," more or less. My talk was given in the Pigeon Forge Library and I was introduced to a fella who was a Sevier County EMT, or emergency technician. Anyway, he drove an ambulance. This was interesting to me at the time because we had just done two stories on the theme "Death, Funerals, and Customs" — the fascinating funeral rituals of our people.

This thirtyish gentleman was talking about traveling back roads and mountain trails, way up near the cow-barn, so to speak. He had traveled way off the beaten path to pick up folks who were seriously ill or even those who had passed away. It was his job, he said, to bring them down out of the mountains and hollers to the hospital emergency room or the funeral home.

It brought to mind that one cold day while Heartlanding when we attended a funeral near the National Park. It was a unique funeral because, in fact, it was one of a hundred cemeteries inside the Park. This cemetery is located way out off of Highway 321, out of Gatlinburg toward Cosby. The funeral was officiated by two different preachers. One of them was Melvin Carr, the "trout whisperer," as he's often called because of his legendary ability to catch mountain trout.

Melvin was preaching, and that's how we heard about the funeral and were able to go and document it. The family was very gracious about our attendance, so we tried to just record it. If I recall correctly, we gave a copy of the video to the grieving family.

The immediate family included about ten adult children along with their families. They ranged in age from babies to folk in their 80s. There were about 70–80 people attending. It was the

51

first time I ever saw the deceased's own family members grab a shovel at the end of the service and cover their loved one with dirt.

The women of the family adjusted and arranged the gravesite flowers before they left. They all took a flower home with them. These folks, dressed nicely in their Sunday-best attire, just went to shoveling and gardening when it was time to do that. Burial and funeral customs are curious. They say a lot about a culture. I've heard this many times during archeological studies: "If you want to know a culture, take a look at their funeral rituals. It will say a lot about a people—how they treat their dead."

Later on, we found out that at the turn of the century when somebody died, the mannerly thing to do was to send cards around to friends and associates of the deceased party to let everyone know the old boy or girl was gone. These business-like cards were scripted in black ink and looked pretty grim, but elegant.

At the time of death, all the clocks in the house were stopped at the precise time of one's passing. Black drapes covered the windows. If it was a child, a lock of hair might be snipped as a keepsake.

We kept hearing that many people were born and died without ever having had their picture taken. That's one reason we see old photographs of the dead, simply because while they were alive they had never had the chance. Somebody wanted to remember them, so the picture was taken after they were dead. It makes perfect sense, particularly if it happened to be a child.

I heard that in Tazewell, or somewhere, a feller died and nobody at the funeral parlor knew much about him. He had no money for a burial, but out of the goodness of the hearts of these kind folks, the embalmers went ahead and fixed him up—at least, they got this poor gentleman *nearly* ready for burial. All the time they worked on him, they were hoping someone would step forward, claim to be some long-lost kin, and provide enough remuneration to bury him.

Well, it never happened. And the embalmed one was stood up, as rigor mortis had set in. He was placed in a back closet somewhere in the maze of catacomb-like hallways and rooms in the funeral home. More than one year passed with that fella left standing up in the back of that closet. I heard this story for the truth. He may be still be there for all I know, waiting for the opportunity to finally be laid to rest instead of standing for all eternity!

In West Knoxville, near Ebeneezer Road and Church, West-land Avenue, and the Blue Grass section of Bearden, there was another burial tale told by folks connected to the Rocky Hill Social Club, or as Jim Dykes would say, "folks of that ilk." Somehow, Tom Gheen was involved with the telling of this tale, though I don't remember if Tom told it himself or if he was just somewhere around while it was being related, or the lie was being spread, however you want to look at it.

Anyway, it involved a couple of rough characters—brothers who lived around the bottoms and flooded areas along the West-land/Ebeneezer section. Supposedly, these boys got in an argument because one of them stole the other's shoes and wore them.

Well, they were so mean that the fella who was wronged just went ahead and shot and killed his brother, "Because he took 'em out and brought 'em back full of mud." Now, I know this to be true because it was told after a discussion about why people sit up all night with the deceased. That one's easy. One reason is to keep the critters and varmints away from the body. Mostly cats, I guess. At least that's what we've been told.

Prior to embalming, the departed might lie out on a pair of sawhorses and a door. Or, perhaps, on a dining-room table if the folks had one, or on a kitchen table or just a plank, whatever they had available. Neighbors would come over, bring food, visit, and tell their favorite nice stories about the dearly departed. They never told any of the bad things the rascal did. At least, not usually at this event unless late in the evening they'd get to drinking and crying about what a good sort he was—even if he really was a polecat who would kill his brother over a pair of shoes. That's low down.

But, back to the story about that West Knoxville ruffian who shot his brother because he wore his shoes and got them muddy. The reason I'm telling you this story is not because of that so much, but because of what happened next. The church cemetery where they went to bury the dead brother was in a boggy area, prone to flooding.

Well, right after they buried this shot-dead brother in a wooden casket, it started to rain. Sure enough, it rained two days straight—hard, frog-strangling rain. Then, in that boggy lowland ground where they had buried him, he floated up and started sailing off downstream toward the creek. Oh, they caught him before he got plumb out to sea—or I guess it'd be the lake here, Fort Loudon Lake. They had to bury him again, maybe two or three times, I don't know, before he stayed buried for good. He was a mean one, kept wanting to pop up.

Now, if Wiley Oakley were telling this story right now, this is when he'd probably yodel. That means it's a tall-tale; maybe not all of it is actually true. But it might be. I heard that this really did happen.

But, let me end this story where it began: with the tale told by the Sevier County ambulance driver, who for years would go up into the mountains and get folks who were sick and bring them to the hospital. If he didn't know what was wrong with them, he'd always just write "DFO" in big letters on the bottom of the chart at the hospital.

After some time, the hospital hired a new emergency-room doctor who didn't know this procedure. Finally, after a while, this doctor asked what "DFO" meant. "Well, sir," the EMT driver related, "when I come up to the mountains to pick up an old timer and ask his wife what's the matter with Uncle Fud, oftentimes, if she doesn't know, she'll just say to me, 'I don't know what's ailing him. He just done fell out.' So, I just write it on the chart—DFO for done fell out!"

Now, I know for a fact this one's true.

Old Balsam

The story of Old Balsam was told to me by Gudger Palmer from North Carolina. Mark Hannah, who was probably the first ranger in the remote Cataloochie area of the National Park, verified it. I'm telling it here for the truth.

Mr. Palmer was an old man when we met him. He was in his 80s and the real deal. He was born and raised in the mountains of Western North Carolina. Most of that time, he called the Cataloochie area his home.

The first Cataloochie rangers lived in remote stations in the Park. Then, as now, it's perhaps the most remote and wild part of the most visited national park. In those early days of the Park, "remote" was as far back into the "back of beyond" as you could get, as Horace Kephart described it in his monumental work on the area and its people, *Our Southern Highlanders.* The area includes the Fontana and Eagle Creek areas, where we saw our first and only panther or cougar, but that, as they say, is another story. If you wanted to go to any place more remote than Cataloochie, you probably had to go to either the Amazon jungle in Brazil or the moon.

I was first introduced to Mark Hanna on the telephone when I called him prior to our visit with Mr. Palmer, and we talked a few times on the phone. We never actually got to meet. One of the things I remember him telling me about was the incredible number of rattlesnakes that once inhabited the Park. He said that when the Park was formed and all those campers, fishermen, and hikers began to arrive in Cataloochie, there was a lot of one-on-one contact with rattlesnakes. After thousands of years, the rattlesnakes of Cataloochie were suddenly forced to share their home with tourists and fishermen, and they didn't like it.

In the early years, from the 1940s through the 1960s, Mark Hannah spent a lot of time trying to keep rattlesnakes and humans separated. Mr. Hannah said they killed nearly ninety rattle-snakes in one season alone. "They were thick in there," Gudger recalled. "Nobody back then considered not killing them, those big six- and eight-foot rattlers. There wasn't much talk about ecology or rattlesnake conservation during those days. Back then, if you got bit, you'd more than likely never make it to a clinic or a hospital in Bryson City or Waynesville, for it was almost an hour away."

The day we met Gudger Palmer, we arranged to meet him near the Waynesville and Maggie Valley exit off Interstate 40. He left his pick-up truck and rode with us in the *Heartland* truck. He assured us we'd make it up and over the mountain into Cataloochie Valley. The Valley is surprisingly similar to Cades Cove. It even looks like it, except it's in North Carolina. Also, it's probably more remote than Cades Cove on the Tennessee side of the National Park.

There's a two-lane, curvy, mostly gravel road leading up, up, up and over the mountain before dropping down into Cata-loochie Valley. Quiet, beautiful, and bowl-shaped, the sprawling valley with open fields and rolling hills spreads before you and is surrounded by 3,500-foot mountains. A crazy thing about it, a most unusual thing, is that road in there. There's a highway running right through the middle of the Cataloochie Valley, the damnedest thing. It's a fine, first-rate, level blacktop, running right through from one side of the valley to the other. It's maybe four miles long.

Once, with wildlife ranger Kim Delozier, we were in Cata-loochie on an elk shoot. We had driven over the mountains to document and videotape the first-ever release of elk back into the wilds of the Great Smoky Mountains National Park. It was a relocation effort that involved many organizations, students, and scientists. It was a damp, misty, spring day and getting colder. As we exited the interstate and started up over the mountain into Cataloochie, sure enough it started snowing. The temperature was about thirty-eight degrees.

All day the temperature dropped. So did the snow. It was one of those spring mountain snowstorms we've always heard about. In no time, the snow was coming down so hard we could dally no longer. We decided to make our hasty retreat no later than

Ranger Kim Delozier, his helper, with Sam Moore and Ernie Engle from WBIR and drugged elk

Heartland cameraman Doug Mills and I with an early Cataloochie elk ready for release

two o'clock. It's a good thing we did, because by three that afternoon the snow was so deep all those left behind were marooned, forced to spend the night trapped in a Cataloochie snowstorm. This included nearly forty students, scientists, and wildlife specialists from all over Tennessee and North and South Carolina.

This is one time we made the right choice and beat it out of there. In a way, I'm sorry we missed the adventure, as I'd like to know what went on that night with all those wildlife animal folks crammed together—what they ate, how they slept, and where. As for us, we were trying to travel in the heart of that snowstorm. It was almost a white out as we spun our tires climbing back out over Cataloochie Mountain. We weren't sure the trusty old *Heartland* truck was going to make it. The snow had already piled up nearly six inches. Remember, this was treacherous going on a good day, and this was *not* a good day. Up, up, and over, whew! We just barely made it.

But this is the tale of Old Balsam and a similar late spring snowstorm that occurred once upon a time in Cataloochie when Gudger Palmer was a boy. This trip with Gudger was our first trip into Cataloochie, so everything was new to us. As we drove along on this gentle spring day, Gudger rode shotgun and identified everything for us—every unique species of tree and shrub, each different wildflower, and all points of interest—as we slowly headed up and over the mountain.

Then, he began reminiscing about the unique forest sounds he had heard as a boy. It was the bells that rang in the forest that he remembered clearest. We had never heard of this before, so we listened carefully. "Bells," he said, "filled the mountains, rang through them, you could hear them all over, everywhere. Each animal had its own specific bell. Hogs, cattle, they all ran free in the mountains. I can still hear those old bells. All of them. But Old Balsam had the prettiest, clearest, and purest sounding bell in all the mountains. Looking up now, I can still hear her bell echoing across them ridges."

It was the first time we'd heard anybody talking about farm animals running free. I had always thought that they were all penned up. Gudger told us different. In the old mountains, before the National Park, split-rail fences were used mainly to keep wild critters and varmints out of your garden. In other words, with the abundance of land, domesticated animals roamed wherever they wanted. If you didn't want them in your corn patch or collard greens patch, you put a fence around it. There was plenty of timber.

An early snow

Shepherds and herders took the animals up to the high mountains, where they fattened up on the new growth and healthy green grasses on the balds in early spring. Salt licks were scattered about and maintained by the herders to keep the animals close. Sometimes, herders would cut notches in old logs and fill them with salt for the cattle and hogs.

As we continued driving along, Gudger started to tell us about Old Balsam. She was a lean, raw-boned, roan cow—the lead cow of a Cataloochie herd in the Great Smoky Mountains. He continued to look out the window. He was seeing something more than we were, something he knew and loved and had called home all his life. As he began to tell us about her, it was as if he could see that old cow again.

"Old Balsam had the sweetest bell sound in all these mountains. Each cow and hog had a bell around its neck. That's what distinguished one critter from the others. That's how they could be found as they roamed free throughout the mountains. With chestnut acorns, big white oaks, beech, there was plenty to eat everywhere. No need to pen them up; you'd just have to provide feed for 'em. It was better to let them roam and feed themselves.

Then, when you needed 'em, you'd just go round 'em up. They'd be all fattened up for you."

We'd heard this also from an older gentleman near Brimstone, Tennessee, who made bells and collected them. He showed us thousands of bells – all shapes and sizes – hanging in his blacksmith shop. There were bells from many different kinds of animals, including, goats, mules, horses, and cattle. Each bell, of course, had its own sound.

But it was the sound of Old Balsam's bell that Gudger Palmer remembered above all others, and we didn't know why. So, we asked him about it. This is the story he told.

He said it took place years ago during early spring. The winter had been the fiercest he could remember, but February and March were unseasonably warm. Although it was earlier than normal, after some discussion, the community decided to go ahead and move the animals up to the high balds where the grass was already rich and green. The stock could then roam free throughout the mountains and would fatten up before returning in the fall.

Old Balsam was the lead cow. Though she was beyond her calf-bearing years, they kept her as the matriarch of the Cataloochie cattle herd. What happened that night was completely unexpected: it began to snow. And it continued to snow for three days, day and night. Gudger Palmer said his father paced the floor all night long. He could hear him from the loft where he slept. His father was worried about the cattle, for he, like everyone else in the community, had everything he owned tied up in his cattle and stock.

On the Sunday morning after those three straight days of snow, the mountains were covered with a two-foot blanket. In spite of the weather, the entire congregation made it to the little white church in Cataloochie that Sunday. The church sat at the end of a long country lane. Fences made of chestnut and cedar rails lined both sides of the long dirt and gravel road leading up to the church.

The late winter blizzard had cut off the herders from their animals. The snow was too deep, and many families thought that the animals, isolated and alone, would eventually freeze to death.

The church in Cataloochie today

Perhaps they could salvage some hides, but that would be all. It was the saddest day anyone in Cataloochie could remember.

However, near the end of the service, the white snow mist began to clear, and some began to wonder if a group of men might be able to reach what was left of the herd after all. But as the members filed out of the church, they noticed something materializing down the lane, as if out of a dream.

They could hear her bell first. Coming down the chestnut lane toward the church was Old Balsam, leading all the other animals with her. As Gudger Palmer told us this story, he had a tear in his eye as he recalled the sound of that old cow and her bell, the loudest, sweetest bell in all the mountains.

We tried for at least a decade to tell this story on *The Heartland Series*, but we never could do it. Although we found a big cow, we never had enough snow to recreate the story of Old Balsam. That's why you may never see it on TV.

Bill's Little Stories

A Tennessee boy arrived on the Vanderbilt campus in Nashville and was looking around for directions when he spied an intelligent looking older man, maybe a professor, in a tweed coat, smoking a pipe. The boy approached the man.

"Hey," he said. "Do you know where the Admissions Office is at?"

The man pulled the pipe out of his mouth, looked the hayseed country boy up and down disapprovingly, and responded, "Son, this is Vanderbilt University. I don't know where you're from, but around here we don't end our sentences with prepositions."

"Well then," the East Tennessean replied, "Do you know where the Admissions Office is at, asshole?"

A Love Story about Sal

On *The Heartland Series*, we didn't do enough love stories. We knew it. Year after year, we continuously tried, with little success, to come up with a Valentine's Day tale for February 14th.

Every year at Christmas, we'd try to get ten days or two weeks off from the pressure of researching, writing, and shooting shows one right after the other. We'd stagger vacations so someone would always be around to man the station and keep the office running. These Christmas vacations usually began around December 18 and ran until after the Wilderness Wildlife event in Pigeon Forge a month later. During this period, the *Heartland* crew was rarely at full strength, so we didn't do much shooting of stories early in January.

Wilderness Wildlife Week in Pigeon Forge was a benchmark for our year. It usually occurred the second week in January, and it always snowed. It served as the true starting point, the beginning of each new season and year. *Heartland* cameraman Doug Mills and I always participated at this very successful winter festival. We'd be featured speakers, have an audience of five-hundred people, show DVDs, and tell our stories. For twenty-four years Doug and I participated in that special celebration of the beauty and wildlife of the Great Smoky Mountains and the National Park. Only after the conclusion of the event did we start working again in earnest.

I always loved those pleasant slow winters. Usually the sky was white for most of late January. Rarely did the sun show its bright face. If it didn't snow a little, it snowed a lot, or was going to. Moisture was in the air. The animals were all hidden away hibernating, and we never could understand why we couldn't do the same.

We'd do an occasional snow show but, usually, we'd spend two weeks in January planning the year and outlining story titles.

We normally went into reruns for a month or had a few stories in the can, which we could air when needed. Often, they were quiet stories with music and didn't require a lot of writing and complicated post-production. The audience liked them and the change of pace.

There were also a million other things to do during this down time, like organizing our scripts, moving tapes into storage, calling our sources and friends to see what they were planning for the year. In other words, we shook the bushes looking for good, new story ideas. We contacted historians, teachers, county extension agents, nurses, hardware and feed-store personnel—anybody who was in contact with people who could recommend good stories. We always checked with our National Park friends to find out what new projects were afoot, particularly in the plant and animal world.

But rarely, if ever, did this research and effort help us find a good Valentine's Day love story. Oh, it might lead to a chance opportunity to shoot a thousand-pound elk mating. But that's not quite the kind of love story we had in mind. We did come across a story about courting once, and we produced it: Wiley Oakley's tale "The Sheep Eye." It involved a boy who gave a sheep's eye to his cute little girl friend. It ended with him walking her home from church. Ha! Some exciting ending, isn't it? Actually, it was, and the show was a hoot, too.

But we rarely found a love story good enough to get excited about. We began to believe we just weren't capable of it. Or perhaps we just didn't have any love in our hearts, which was even worse! We were just about ready to take this fault with us to the grave. Then, we would have been forever known as the "Heartless *Heartland* Crew" who never learned to understand love.

That's why when Sam Moore, the *Heartland* editor, first spoke about a love-story lead he was working on, we thought, "Yippidy doo da!" Maybe now, at last, we might be able to explore our feminine side, the emotional core where love hangs out. Well, maybe we weren't thinking that way exactly or that far ahead, either. We were just glad we had a lead. That, for us, was a miracle of rare device and cause for celebration.

Sam had been talking at length on the telephone with an older gentleman named Connie Boling from Oak Ridge. Connie spent his early years in rural Virginia. He was a very happy man in his 90s and full of life. He related to Sam how, as a young man, certain things happened to him while he was courting his girlfriend Sal at her cabin across the mountains. The story he told was named "Daylight Courtin'."

"It was easy to court at night," he began enthusiastically, "but courtin' in the daytime was a different thing entirely. First off, her brothers and father were around, usually."

Connie related his tale with the matter-of-fact, full confidence of one who knew what he was speaking about. You might say he had a graduate degree and much experience in life-lessons. He spoke with a twinkle in his eye and a song and dance in his heart. What topped it off for us was that we never knew if he was pulling our leg just a little bit or not. Doug Mills (who shot the show and the interview), Sam Moore, and I believe Connie Boling had more fun telling the story than anybody could possibly have had listening to it.

"You couldn't get any courtin' done with her brothers around or her daddy either. That's for sure," he said. "I had to walk about three miles or more over the mountains to Sal's place to get to see her. I was a-sweatin' pretty heavy, too, when I finally arrived. I could see Sal's maw out front of the cabin. It looked like she had a rifle-gun in her hands, too, lookin' out for me a-comin' — just a-waitin' for me!

"No, on second thought, it wasn't a rifle-gun after all. It was a broom. I could see it as I got closer." Connie described how the cabin lay in a pretty little valley with a garden right outside the porch and a big cornfield nearby.

"But, Maw was good to me, and invited me to come on inside. She said that Sal would be ready in a minute. She gives me some cool water to drink, which tasted mighty fine after my long trek over the mountains. I was a-settin' when I heard Sal holler down from the loft upstairs for her maw to bring her shoes up. So, Sal's maw picked up her shoes and said to me that she was going to take them up to Sal in the loft, which was right above where I was settin' in front of the fireplace."

Connie explained that to do this, "Maw had to climb the wall." We'd never come across this phrase before, and didn't know what it meant. All these old cabins, we learned, had lofts, and Connie was referring to climbing up the side of the cabin into the loft by way of an opening between the floors. Usually, the opening was against the wall. Short poles or long pegs were driven into the logs and stuck out from the wall. They were used as rungs, like you would use a ladder.

"Maw climbed the wall to give Sal her shoes. Climbin' up, climbin' up, climbin' up!"

What happened next was "the hook" in the story and a huge surprise.

"As I was sitting there a-waitin' for Sal to get dressed and listening, I could hear Sal a-movin around above me. Sort of a-rumblin' around. The more she moved dressing, the more the puncheon floor boards rattled around. All of a sudden, the boards popped up and Sal came falling down through the floorboards with a big boom. She crashed down onto the floor in front of me. She landed on her bottom at my feet with a surprised look on her face. Me? I just stared down at her with her a-lookin' up at me!

"All she was wearin', all the clothes she had on in this world, was this little piece of material that covered her across here." He motioned to his chest area to signify her breasts. "It was a makeshift brassiere, I guess. I'd never seen one, as girls didn't wear things like that in those days. That's all she wore. That's all she had on!" Connie said with a smile.

"Well, when Sal hit the ground, she looked at me surprised-like, and I looked right back at her. Then, she popped up and bolted out the door as fast as she could go! And she could run fast, too."

I asked Connie what he did then.

He said, "I jumped up and ran right out the door after her. I chased her as fast as I could go. When she got outside off the porch, she run across a little yard at a dead run. Then, she turned up into the cornfield and headed up between the wide rows."

"What did you do then?" I asked.

Connie laughed. "I ran after her," he said. "And she could run fast, too. And all she had on was a smile! I was running through that cornfield as fast as I could go and wasn't gaining an inch on her at all. Then, I looked to my side, and there, running next to me, was Maw, keeping right up, stride-for-stride and following Sal. Then her maw yells out to her real loud, 'Change rows, Sal!'"

There was a long pause. We all just looked at each other. We couldn't believe it. But then we couldn't stop laughing. Connie told this to us on-camera, of course. When he was finished, he just smiled and, after getting all worked up telling the story, he just eased himself back against his sofa. As he did, I asked him what happened next. After a pause, he said, still smiling: "I went home." It was the perfect end to his story.

As we packed up our gear, went outside, and slushed through January's ice and snow, we all knew Connie's story would make a great *Heartland* episode. But we also knew it wasn't going to happen any time soon. It certainly wouldn't be ready for Valentine's Day this year. Maybe next year. Ha! But the biggest reason for the delay, which was crystal clear to all of us, was that to do the story, more than anything else we needed a mature cornfield. We had six months to get this story ready, because it would be at least August before corn would be high enough to hide a naked girl running through it.

Sure enough, the following August, we had a script. So, armed with actors and permission to use a huge cornfield in Townsend behind the Heritage High School, we shot "Daylight Courtin'."

In the spring, about four months earlier, I had met a tall, freckle-faced, cute fourteen-year-old girl. I think she was the niece of one of my neighbors, Ronnie Boone. She was from Florida, spending the summer with her cousins and relatives in East Tennessee. She was a perfect choice for the part of Connie's girl, Sal. All I had to do was get permission from her uncle to let us take pictures of her naked running through a cornfield! That'll be easy, huh? How's that for a simple request? Of course, she'd be wearing skin-colored tights and shorts. It was all in good fun, no problem!

We had a great talent to play young Connie Boling, a young Mr. Shaad from the University of Tennessee's Theater Department. Gail Green played Sal's mother, and we had a ten-year-old boy driving a four-wheeler while Doug shot from atop the back of it. They drove up and down, back and forth along the corn rows to get the truck-shots of actors running through the cornfield. That ten-year-old kid could really drive that thing, too. He brought Doug and the camera right up alongside Maw and young Connie chasing after Sal. It looked like a Bugs Bunny cartoon with Wile E. Coyote running in place with that goofy music in the background. Then, she takes off fast and runs out of frame—whoooosh! Maw really did look like Wiley Coyote running after Sal.

It worked great and looked great. Doug shot until we got it right. A professional, high-priced stunt driver couldn't have done any better than that little boy, driving Doug around all day. We shot the cabin part of the story at the Museum of Appalachia. Then, when Sal ran out across the yard, we cut to a shot in the Townsend cornfield. It was a huge thirty- to fifty-acre cornfield. It was beautiful, too: tall, ripe, and green.

We wanted to see a wide shot of young Connie, Sal, and Maw running through the cornfield. But we also needed to see the Smoky Mountains behind the cornfield. To do this, we had to move and re-set up at a neighbor's cornfield, instead of the one we had been using for medium length and tight shots. The neighbors were friendly and generously agreed to allow us to go through their cornfield on the day of the shoot. We tried not to tear it up much. But, there was one big problem. Though the corn looked great, when we walked down into it to set up the shot, we got lost. We actually did.

The corn was nearly fourteen-feet high. We'd never seen such a large field of corn. We couldn't communicate back and forth with Doug. That was the problem. We spent an hour-and-a-half trying to find our way through that cornfield. All you can see in the shot is the corn wiggling as somebody or something moves through it. With the Smoky Mountains in the background, it was a beautiful shot, thanks to Doug. As the director, I was lost in there with the actors in the corn. You couldn't see me though; you couldn't see them, or anything. We had no idea corn grew so high. That was the final shot of the day, as Connie is saying, "I went home. That was a great adventure."

What a wonderful day and a wonderful, memorable episode. "Daylight Courtin'" was just one of those special stories, one big, happy barrel of monkey shines from start to finish. It was a joy to work on it. It was like a sundae with a cherry on top! Like Ode Reagan said, "It was a pleasure, a real pleasure."

This little tale had evolved into a beautiful full-reenactment, including the use of actors, costumes, and on-location filming.

It spanned almost our entire region, reaching from Happy Valley in the southern end of the National Park, across Chilhowee Mountain to Townsend, where we shot on-location on a farm near Heritage High School. We traveled across the Tennessee Valley to Oak Ridge for the interview with Connie and to the Museum of Appalachia in Norris, Tennessee, where we also shot parts of the story.

Sometimes stories just work out. Usually, you get out of a story what you put into it. In the case of "Daylight Courtin'," the whole was a lot more than the sum of its individual pieces. This sweet little episode turned out to be everything we had hoped and more. Even today, more than a decade later, just thinking about young love and the actors in this story produces a warm and fuzzy feeling in me. After doing nineteen-hundred *Heartland* episodes, I can still say that this one was special, one of my personal favorites. As to why is difficult to answer.

One possible answer, as the oracle might pause to say, is "It's just a wonder." Or, another answer might be found in another producer's line. In the film *Shakespeare in Love*, when asked straight out how it all happened, the goofy producer answers with the same phrase he's always used to describe the chaos of the theater—"It's a miracle!"

On this particular story we had a great group of actors, and our production team worked well with them. Folks at different locations were cooperative and generous from start to finish, both onscreen and off. The weather was great.

There are so many intangibles in a production, and each has to work out well for the entire episode to be successful. For instance, in this story we had to include a particular person as an actor. He got to portray a minor character because he had made a donation at a fundraiser. Now, think about that. How crazy is that? The odds of this working out, that this person would be helpful and contribute, not to mention be able to act, aren't very good. But, luckily, he was.

Sometimes, though, even when everything works better than hoped for, things do not work out. The story just doesn't come off for one reason or another. It might be the story. Or maybe it's the casting, or the direction, or the costumes, or the wrong location, or too much background noise, or it keeps raining, or a million other things. Maybe one of the actors is a pain in the ass, or the director for some reason is hung over, or sick, or stupid! Maybe we got lost, or couldn't get any lunch, or couldn't find a tape, or the camera acted up. Perhaps we didn't have enough money in the budget, or we traveled too far and ran out of time.

One time, we were working on a story about the Christmas of 1838 during the Trail of Tears. It was a story called "The Discovery." We had some great actors, and lots of them. We also had great locations. But we weren't able to catch the horse in its pasture the day of the shoot. A major character, the captain, was supposed to ride that horse in all his scenes. Well, he couldn't, because we couldn't catch it. But we had to go on and shoot the story anyway, so we just filmed the captain walking with his men, instead of riding his horse. It looked a little like a scene from *Monty Python and the Holy Grail.* Fortunately, this didn't hurt the story very much. It only hurt the feelings of the actor who was supposed to be riding the horse. He was extremely pissed off. However, this didn't ruin the production, because in the story the captain was the bad guy anyway, and people enjoyed disliking him as a character. So, it worked.

Maybe, above all else, the single reason "Daylight Courtin'" was so successful was because of Mr. Connie Boling himself. Connie often called the studio and always wanted to talk to Sam, who had been the first one of us he spoke with when he first called. Sam was the one he wanted to talk to about everything; he was Connie's particular friend from the beginning through the eight months it took to complete the story. Connie Boling was one happy dude. Any time we had the privilege of spending time visiting with Connie, he was always a joy to be around.

The Ballad of Pirate Paddy O'Dea

I started writing this story at Sunset Beach, South Carolina, and finished it on a cold rainy day last fall while selling books at Robert Tino's Fall Festival in Sevierville.

Since I'm half Irish, I thought it would be fun to write about a one-armed, one-legged Irish pirate who sailed the coasts of North and South Carolina.

After years of visiting Charleston, Pauley's Island, Litchfield, and Myrtle Beach, I've come to appreciate the pirates who once sailed the seas from these areas. I'm particularly interested in sea-faring ghost tales and sea adventurers.

I imagined a love-sick Irish pirate who has fallen in love with a fine Charleston Lady. Consider this tale as a humorous, swashbuckling, South Carolina ghost story or a rousing, drinking song performed, perhaps, by the great Irish band The Pogues. (See a depiction of the pirate in the color photo gallery, Plate 18).

BE YE OF LAND,
BE YE FROM SEA,
The ballad of Paddy O'Dea, this I'll be.
FE FI FO FUM, I smell the blood of an Irishman . . . .

It was a terrible night,
a horrible dreary sight,
the first full moon in June.
Daylight came none too soon.
Wet critters caught out. Wolves slain,
their putrid coats sloshing in the rain.
Wolves howled: A –WOOOOOOO!

Waves crashed against rocks. The misty-mist blew bones
across the heath; the whistling wind, slap, slap, slap,
shutters on broken hinges echoing back, clippity-clap.
"Lost souls rise on nights like this," the boatswain squalled.

Wraiths ride, slashing black night apart;
Shimmering coats shake . . . drip, dripping, sopping;
Creaking, stretching, long oars snap, and
splatter against reefs as a huge, sallow ship docks.
Out steps Paddy stripped to the waist,
stub of his left arm leather-manacled to a dagger
a-hanging from it. He's a madman for all or nothing!

Born of a wench in a good strong stench
at Boarshead Tavern, Greyfair Town.
She traded him to a bum for a keg of rum.
So off to sea he did flee with blanket,
bottle, musket, and gun.

From grace he trod and faith in God,
toward evil he did run.

Witches and wenches and killings 'n such,
the lad swore the oath from those he knew:
Blackards and Swedes, lawless and grave,
shipmates and bunkmates, both evil and brave.

In Dorchester town, a husband came home,
and finding Paddy there,
slashed off his arm and parted his hair
with the cutlass he'd left by his clothes on the chair.

Later, when he lost a leg,
he wore a peg
which went rat-a-tat-tat across the deck
to the yardarm where he'd stretch yer neck!

So you better jump and be ready fer mean ole Paddy
should he an order give,
or he'll keel haul ye, 'n heads 'ill swing,
ere his dagger 'ill be in yer ribs!

Her name was Peg to match his leg,
ginger and rare, voluptuous and fair.
Paddy stole her in a dressing gown
from a one-eyed Lord in Charleston Town.

She loved him, though no man knows
what she saw in him or cared.
He loved her, too, fer Peg was true,
and to ole Paddy her bosom she bared.

But a woman at sea, meant trouble to be.
Paddy knew only too well.
At Sunset Beach, he set her free,
though he'd sooner sail in hell.

At night she roams the dunes till dawn,
her bosom bared for thee.
Ole Paddy mourns that Peg is gone,
no more their love will be.

When she told me this yarn, I sure was drawn.
She remains a mate to be,
to live and wander and lay 'till dawn,
and share her bed with me!

Bill's Little Stories

A feller from Kentucky, probably a Harlan County native, and a friend of cameraman Doug Mills, was driving south into Tennessee one time when he got pulled over by a Tennessee state trooper. The trooper walked up to the car and asked the man if he had any I.D.?

"About what?" he replied.

Reed and Creed Kirkland

I want to tell you about one of the real natives of these parts, my friend Creed Kirkland. Like A.D. Bohanon once said talking about Walter, his brother, "He's been living here nigh on over seventy years. I reckon he's been here long enough to be called one of the natives."

Sitting quietly in the corner of Blount and Monroe Counties is the home community of one of the genuine, legitimate, real mountain characters still alive today. Creed Kirkland lives near Pumpkin Center, where Highway 72 intersects with Highway 129. If that road, 129, sounds familiar, it's because it's also called "The Tail of the Dragon," a famous stretch of curvy road where there are 318 curves in eleven miles. Motorcyclists occasionally get killed on it. It crosses the Tennessee/North Carolina state line and lies near the southern boundary of the Great Smoky Mountains National Park, not too far from Chilhowee Dam and the mouth of Citico Creek. It's the upper reaches of the Tellico Reservoir, what used to be the Little Tennessee River but is now a lake.

Not too long ago this was remote, wild country. To many people, it is still. Creed's home is actually only about five miles, as the crow flies, from both the mouths of Abrams Creek and Citico Creek. These streams just happen to be two of the purest freshwater streams in the entire world, not just in North America.

This is why the Native Americans lived here. It's the home territory of the Overhill Cherokees, and along the Little Tennessee River there are actually underwater remains of ten Native American villages. It's also why house lots in Tellico Village sell for well over $100,000 per acre. The Yankees and Snowbirds are here for the same reasons the Cherokee were: spectacularly beautiful country, pure water, and abundant game.

I first met Creed cleaning up brush near the site of my future

Creed and giant mussel caught
on a fishing pole

house. Jerry Hughes was helping me build a cabin home next to the National Park, and Creed was helping Jerry with this hard, hot work. There he was, this little old man with a scraggly beard and bad legs. He was in his early 70s then and was throwing brush around a lot faster than me.

His story and his family's history and bloodline go hand-in-hand with this fairly wild country. Creed's clan is the direct descendant of "Guerrilla" Kirkland, the famous Civil War bushwhacker. Kirkland and his band of brigands terrorized these mountains and their people during the War of Northern Aggression. Supposedly, there is a monument to him, somewhere near Deals Gap, up near the North Carolina /Tennessee border. Mr. Kirkland, Creed's father, once ran the ferry across the Little Tennessee River near Tallassee General Store. It was just downstream a few thousand yards below where Chilhowee Dam is now. The ferry, which of course is no longer there, was located a bit upstream from ole Hoss Holt's store, which doesn't mean a thing to you, unless you're from these parts or have the memory of an elephant.

Ed Decker, my neighbor, told a story that occurred when he visited the Kirkland's place nearly fifty years ago when he was seventeen years old. He said he and Creed are about the same age and grew up in the same neck of the woods. Ed said he stumbled through cars parked in high grass, some with motors in them, most without. They were parked in the bushes and weeds in the front yard. Ed said he made it inside the house where Creed's father was sitting without shoes.

Just as Mr. Kirkland stood up and invited Ed to breakfast, a big roach ran across the floor. Mr. Kirkland quickly stepped on it with his bare foot and crunched it. Ed declined breakfast, but here's the thing: Ed says that when he came toward the house, he passed a passel of young boys, all about teenager-age. Four or five of them came crawling out of these cars where they had been sleeping. That's not all. At the same time, Ed said four or five of the prettiest girls he ever saw were coming out of the bedrooms in the house, one right after the other. They were all the Kirkland girls, Creed, and Reed's sisters.

Creed told me a friend once came over to wish his family a Merry Christmas. As was the custom then, he brought his hog rifle, fired it in the air, and hollered out, "Christmas Gift." Everyone in Creed's family rushed outside to welcome the neighbor and give him a Christmas cookie, or whatever little treat they had for him. This was way before people started giving each other Christmas presents, though they knew about St. Nick and the newer Christmas traditions. At this time, Christmas was just another day.

Creed had a house full of sisters, six of them, and one of them stumbled outside during this Christmas greeting and got a whiff of a dead dog that prior to its demise had taken refuge nearby. Well, Creed said his sister cried all Christmas long, both day and night, because she thought the neighbor man had actually put an end to old St. Nick. She cried, "That man done killed Santa Claus."

This is Creed's country. He knows it and everything about it. I didn't know his brother, Reed, but I've heard Creed and many other local folks tell wild tales about their hunting escapades, both separate and together. And I'm aiming to share some of them with you for the truth.

One story I heard at the Fast Lap convenience and gas station at Lanier has to do with the survival instincts of black bears. It seems Reed was always on the hunt for a bear and usually would be the one to climb the tree and get it out. Well, on this particular hunt, supposedly there was a newbie or a rookie bear hunter with them. So, when they treed the bear, this other feller volunteered to climb the tree after it. It was a job normally undertaken with pride by Reed, or so I've been told.

When knocked out of a tree, a bear will usually run up hill. So, if you're watching or standing around when a bear is knocked out of a tree, you want to be on the downhill side. You do NOT

Bears in tree

want to be on the trail or in front of a 500-pound bear when he decides to run uphill! Of course, it's all downhill to a black bear anyway.

Well, as the story goes, Reed was standing around, a bit angry because he didn't get to climb the tree after the bear. So Reed wasn't paying much attention, and when the bear came out of the tree, he took off a-runnin'. Reed wasn't in too safe a spot, and the bear just plumb up and run over him. Of course, he wasn't hurt, or not too bad, for you couldn't hurt those boys. They were tough as pine knots.

Before we go too much further, I need to say that for folks near the National Park fifty years ago, poaching was a way to feed a clan the size of the Kirklands, growing up poor in purse

Reed, giant turkey, and Harvey Garland

though rich in a lot of other ways. I try not to make judgments about what happened long ago and encourage you, dear reader, to do the same–especially if you continue to read this and are at all interested in some of these wild hunting and living stories.

Creed himself told me about the big buck that they thought they'd killed who came back to life. He told me this with that funny kind of sly smile of his. Creed said they'd shot it and were putting it in the trunk of their car to sneak it back home to clean and eat it.

However, just as they were trying to stuff the big buck deer into the trunk of the car, they heard another car coming right toward them. Creed said he quickly jumped into the trunk with the dead buck and tried to hold the trunk lid slightly open. Instead, he jerked the lid, and it locked tight. Now Creed was locked in the trunk, and that's when the big dead buck woke up. It wasn't dead!

Both Creed and the buck started banging around, trying to get Reed or whoever was driving to stop the car and let them out. The deer started kicking Creed in his chest. It had awakened fussing and angry and wanting to know what it was doing in the trunk of an old car racing down Highway 129.

Creed, the hunter

Another time, they had a big buck in the back of a pick-up truck, one of those trucks with the sliding-glass panel behind the driver's head. It seems the deer in the back of the truck hadn't gone to heaven after all. Instead, as they were driving home and feeling good about the meat they had for the family to share, the old critter came back to life. That big buck just stood up while the truck was haulin' ass down the Tail of the Dragon. So, they opened the sliding-glass window and dispatched it; just pointed the rifle-gun through the truck window and shot the buck again. Creed said, "He laid right back down this time, where he should have stayed in the first place!"

I'm not condoning any illegal activities or even some that are merely borderline bad deeds. No sir, I'm just reporting on or pointing out what it might take for some folks to survive – how in the not-too-distant past they learned to make a living and survive in the wild country around the southern boundary of the Great Smokies.

Those boys, Creed and Reed, were legendary bear hunters. They were scrappers of the highest order – mountain boys who

Skinning bears

turned into mountain men about 150 years too late for their time. Creed and Reed, both barefoot, would often scale a sixty-foot white oak or white pine with a tire-iron to knock a bear out of the tree. This, of course, happened after their dogs had treed it. Creed was near thirty years old before he ever hunted with shoes on. That's what I've heard from more than one source. Creed, too, told me that, and he told it for the truth.

It's well known that one of Creed's dogs once swam Chilhowee Lake after some critter. As Creed watched from one side of the lake by the bank, a bunch of hunters appeared on the other side, coming out of nowhere. And no sooner had they appeared than they started mistreating and kicking Creed's dog. Well, that just ain't done. So, after hollering and screaming at them without any results, Creed immediately stripped naked as a jay-bird and jumped into the freezing lake and took off swimming across it after his dog. And he did this with his big hunting knife locked tight between his teeth.

He swam the entire Chilhowee Lake in the winter with a Bowie knife between his teeth. But, by the time Creed made it out of the water on the other side, the hunters were gone. It was a good thing, too. So, there was nothing else for Creed to do except stand tall and naked and wave back across the lake to the boys on the other side who were holding his clothes. Then he swam back.

I never met or knew Reed, I'm sorry to say, but I hear Reed was pretty wild and famous in his own right. Creed did tell me they used to hunt everywhere together. Creed said that once when he was hunting with Reed, they decided to split up and meet later. It wasn't long before Creed found himself caught in a tight spot. He was crawling through thick rhododendron on his belly, following a bear track, when he came face-to-face with a great big rattlesnake. It looked him square in the eye. The spot was so tight Creed couldn't reach his rifle-gun, which was on his back. He only had his left hand free in front of him. So, Creed reached out and grabbed that snake by the neck. Then, with his right hand, he took out his knife from his boot and cut off the snake's head and threw it in his pack.

Well, according to Creed, when he met up with Reed later, Reed said he was starving and asked him if he had anything to eat. So, Creed just threw down the pack and said he thought there were some crackers in it. "You can have 'em. He'p yourself, Reed!" Reed fished around in the pack looking for crackers or something until he came across this big rattlesnake! He didn't know it was dead, and so he started screaming. "Then, he came after me! He would a-killed me if he could have caught me," Creed said, laughing.

Ed Decker said that back when they were seventeen years old or thereabouts, Creed always hung around the little restaurant in Pumpkin Center where Creed's Aunt Artie looked after him some. You know, took care of him. Creed had a jeep and a fifty-pound bag of dog food and some molasses and honey. With these supplies for his dogs, he took off one day and started up the mountain, but he turned the jeep over. He came back with dog food and molasses all over him and Aunt Artie and Creed's cousin, Evalika Canon, tried to wash it out in the sink in the restaurant. I asked Creed if that was true. He smiled and sheepishly said, "Every time after that, fer a long while, whenever I combed my hair, I fed my dogs."

He still has plenty of dogs, maybe twenty up the holler where he lives. Sometimes, in spring, you can see him coming out of the brush on the side of the road with a fishing pole. Or, in the fall, he'll be on the side of the road with the other bear hunters listening for sounds from their dogs.

After a fishing trip last week, I went by the Last Lap convenience store in Lanier for a cup of coffee. It's Creed's stomping ground and I thought I might catch him there. Sure enough, in a drizzle, Creed was walking into the store just ahead of me. He said he found a few more family pictures, including a photo of his dad, and he had another bear hunting photo or two. We sat in a booth looking them over when Creed started in on this fishing tale.

It seems he was trout fishing once below Hoss Holt's place on the old "Little T" Tennessee River near where Chilhowee dam is located now. Creed said he and Hoss didn't see eye to eye on many things and this day old Hoss called the game warden on Creed.

Creed was fishing wearing full body waders, the kind that comes up to your chest. He was catching trout one right after another. Finally, when he looked up he saw the game warden watching him. Creed had his fish stringer around his neck but up until then he was putting the trout in his waders. When he saw the game warden, he started putting the trout on the stringer. When the game warden turned his head, he'd drop another fish down into his waders. He'd put one on the stringer to every two he'd drop in his waders; it went like that.

But, when Creed started out of the river, the warden came up to him and told him he needed to take off his waders. Creed said, "No." He thought he'd just go on home and take them off there, because he was cold. The game warden told him again that he needed to go ahead and take them off. Creed said he'd rather not. "No," the game warden said, "you need to take them off now!"

Well, Creed had 101 trout in his waders. I guess they all went to flopping on the ground. But, Creed wasn't too worried because he knew the particular judge he would face in court. The fine was normally about $45.00 per fish above the legal limit of seven trout.

When Creed's case came up in court the judge started off by saying that "Creed had a big family with eleven or twelve mouths to feed." When he heard that from the judge, Creed knew it looked pretty good for him. They ended up charging him $45.00 for all 101 fish. Since he had paid for them, Creed then asked the judge if he could have the fish. The judge told the warden to go ahead and clean all the fish and put them on ice for Creed.

One other thing, Creed offered to pay another $45.00 if the game warden would clean another hundred fish for him and he asked the judge if that was okay, too! Creed never told me if the judge agreed or not. He just laughed all the while he was telling me about it.

Once, on the trail of a huge European wild boar in the winter, Creed had tracked it across the frozen ice of Tab Cat Creek. When Creed hit the ice and started across, it broke and he fell through. He held up that night under a rock ledge and covered himself in leaves to keep from freezing to death. The next day, as the search party was heading out to look for him, Creed came walking home in eight inches of snow not too much the worse for wear. He was barefooted.

The bench sitters at the Last Lap convenience store in Lanier told me this last tale. However, I have my doubts about its authenticity. Supposedly, Creed got mad once and took some dynamite with him to fish below Chilhowee dam. When he lit the fuse, they said he had set it too close, and he blew the whole dam up, everything went sky high. It was so huge an explosion that every last piece of brick, block, and mortar went straight up in the air. When it did, they said you could see the river running under it. Then, when the entire dam came back down with a gigantic crash and boom, each brick landed back down exactly the way it was before Creed blew it up.

I guess that's why that dam has always leaked a bit to this day.

Mountain Speech

Ever since my college days and for most of my life, I've been personally interested in language. Actually, as an actor and director, it's been part of my business. Whether as an actor creating and portraying characters or as a director directing them, it's about how people talk. It involves what is said and why, speaking patterns, words, phrases, etc. In short, it's the language of specific people. Many great scholars, wonderful writers, and educators have passed along much of what I'm sharing here.

Like most things, people choose to work at what they have a knack for or are particularly good at. Usually we've been introduced to our interest by a great teacher or mentor. Like Effie Baker, a *Heartland* subject who shared with us the story of "Joney and the Whale," used to say, "We were born to it, or raised to it." If we weren't, we picked it up because of a great teacher along the way. Dr. John Tinkler, Linguistic Professor at the University of Tennessee at Chattanooga, is the person most responsible for getting me through college.

Charlotte Ross from the Appalachian State University Appalachian Studies Program first introduced me to many of these ideas about language in the programs we did with her in the early years of *The Heartland Series*. Among other things, she said, "It's not that we aren't using rules of language in the way we talk, but here in the Southern Appalachians, we are using older rules." She used this sentence as an example: "The tree done blowed down." The word "done" is used for emphasis. But "blowed" is the past participle of the verb "blow," and it was used and accepted as correct until 1920 or thereabouts. At that time, the conjugation of the verb blow was "blow," "blowed," "blowed." There was little use of the word "blew" until after 1920.

Dr. Cratis Williams of Berea College in Kentucky spent his life documenting and explaining these unique characteristics and

Black Will Walker poses with one of his three wives

origins of Southern mountain speech. His monumental book of the same name is an exciting and fascinating document. I believe he was the first to identify and accept Southern mountain speech for what it is—the language of his people. Basically, he argues that the way we talk isn't wrong, which was a revolutionary suggestion at the time he wrote it. He sought to explain the origin of our speech and to trace specific words back to their country of origin. It's that linguistic step that we continue to use today to better understand where our speech comes from.

If I may paraphrase a bit, Dr. Williams explains that mountain people speak with their chins up and forward, "much like the mountaineer faces each day with his chin up and face into the wind." And it's also because of our penchant for using the letter "r" whenever we can. I'll discuss this later.

How Come We Talk the Way We Do?

Southern mountain speech is the language of the pioneer. There are as many different dialects as there are hills and hollers in Southern Appalachia. For our purposes we'll combine them all under the general term "Southern mountain speech." It's how we talk here.

Back to the question in the title, and it is a great question: "How come we talk the way we do?" I'm going to try to answer, but first, isn't it interesting that we don't ask, "Why do we talk the way we do?"

You see, already we're introducing historical reasons to answer our speech question. Yes, historical and cultural factors invade our speech all the time. As a group of people who talk in a certain manner, folks from Southern Appalachia don't often use the word "why." First off, we just don't like it. Secondly, we would rather say "How come" than "why." We'd rather use two words instead of one.

Dr. Cratis Williams of Berea College was one of the first people to study and write about how we talk in Appalachia. He coined the term "Southern mountain speech" and explains that mountain people don't like to use words that require the use of the back of our throats, words like "why" and "where," for instance. Instead, we'd rather speak using our teeth and lips. That's why we prefer to say "how come."

We also prefer the 'm' sound in "come." Now, say "why" and think about the difference. When we say "why," everything happens in the back of our mouths and we are forced to smile, which we don't like to do. We also have to open our mouths to do it and we don't like to do that either. Similarly, we'd rather say "tar" than "tire" and "far" instead of saying "fire."

We're all aware of the amazing variety of ways Americans have of speaking English. Although we use the English language, we speak "American." In other words, we speak American English, whatever that is. The variety of dialects across America varies from region to region, state to state, even county to county. Many more dialects are separated by geographic or economic boundaries, which tend to create and maintain speech patterns and the similarities and differences among them.

For instance, folks on this side of the mountain may say "hy-ere," while folks on the other side may say "here." If you ask them how come, they generally say that's the way it's always been.

But again, we'll collectively refer to all these dialects as Southern mountain speech, because although the actual dialect may vary, many of the words and phrases are common. The lilt, inflection, special intonation, or other unique characteristics separating one Southern mountain dialect from another are generally minor compared to their similarities.

Folks along the Cumberland Plateau speak slightly different from folks from Lookout Mountain, near Chattanooga. But, they also speak very different from folks in Memphis or Boston. Near Jamestown, Tennessee, they talk different from the folks in and around Roane Mountain, near Elizabethton and Johnson City. We all know and understand this.

All along the Appalachian Mountains, anywhere folks from the British Isles settled, there remain remnants of the old mother tongue, the language of our forefathers. Linguists say that we are more likely than ever before to deliberately hold on to some of these sayings and unique ways of speaking, regardless of education. This use of language – *our* language – is inbred in us, and we may or may not even be conscious of it. However, more than ever before, we are consciously choosing to speak the way "our people" have always talked, to hold on to it. This is a relatively new turn of events and has only begun to happen in the last thirty years or so.

For instance, some folks save or collect antiques like a two-hundred-year-old pie safe or, perhaps, a watch that once belonged to old Grand Pap. The way we speak is far more personal than an object. It's more a part of our being, more an actual part of who we are and where we've come from.

Linguists say many people are aware of these unique turns of phrases and ways of talking, and they are reluctant to change or give up these connections to the past and their families. It may remind them of the ole home place, or simply of family memories. Other folks may feel that changing their language would force them to be untrue or even treasonous toward their tribe and clan.

If we do change, and discard some of these old sayings that have been used and passed down for generations, we may feel we are giving up something of great value. We may do it hesitantly. We may even feel some guilt for doing it. We are who we are and who our people have always been. If we consciously change, then we are not the same. It goes without saying.

At times throughout history it has been necessary to discard these old forms of speech. Many felt they had to in order to move up the social and economic pecking order. For generations, Southern mountain people have been encouraged, if not forced, to learn to speak like the rest of American English speakers. We were trained to speak like everyone else by well-intentioned English teachers and then further encouraged by our colleagues, friends, and peers, particularly people we admired.

Recently, however, many more of us than ever before, thank goodness, have chosen to retain our dialects and way of speaking, which is as unique to our mountains and its people as are our individual dipping gourds. In our current language lie the remnants of an older language, the one the pioneers used when America was first settled.

I remember once talking to Mr. Cooper, a millstone sharpener in Rennie, Tennessee, who was showing us his blacksmith shop. He was talking about his bellows and explaining how it operated. As he did, he pointed to his "har," as he called it.

"Pardon me?" I said, not understanding.

"The har, hyere. I'm talking about the har!" he explained, yelling even louder.

After a pause, I asked, "What's a har?"

"A har!" he said, exasperated. "A har! You know, A HAR!"

I later learned that he was talking about a hearth, but I couldn't understand him.

After asking three times, I was too ashamed to admit that I didn't know what he was talking about—more specifically, what he was saying. I didn't want to ask again. I didn't want to insult Mr. Cooper by showing my ignorance, so although I couldn't understand his answer, I let the issue pass. Wars are fought and entire countries lost, I suspect, for much the same reason: the inability of people to understand one another.

It's true that fifty-seven percent of all people who originally settled in the Southern Appalachians were from the British Isles. Unlike today, when we used to hear old sayings, we intuitively knew or understood that they originated back home in the old country. Here is a frequent example, used in this case by Ray Hicks, a Boone, North Carolina, mountain storyteller: "You've

Jack Huff heading to Mt. LeConte

a man. You hope me out." Using the word "hope" as the past tense of "help" was common in the days of Chaucer. It's middle-English usage, perhaps one of the few remaining in use today.

Charlotte Ross says that because we are familiar with Shakespeare as an old language, we immediately think Southern mountain speech goes back to the language of Shakespeare. We do that simply because we're familiar with it, but, generally, that's not always the case, as we've learned since our initial story on language, "Our Native Tongue," first aired in 1985.

Since then, we've done about four language stories and stud-

Little Lucinda Oakley Ogle

ies, with the help of many producers, writers, and scholars, particularly Dr. Michael Montgomery and his work *Dictionary of Smoky Mountain Language.* Dr. Montgomery and other linguists have traced words, sayings, and their uses not just back to the old country, the British Isles, but to the specific country where each saying or word originated: Scotland, England, Ireland, or Wales.

Many Southern folks say, "You all" (or "y'all"). Those words first appeared together in the King James Bible, "ye" + "all" as "you all." Therefore, it's an English trait to say "you all." Johnny Ray Hicks of Jamestown, Tennessee, once said to us, "You've seen people who can read a book, but they ain't got no learnin' at all, ain't ye?" He's using "ye" for "you," which is also an English trait. Dr. Montgomery identified this trait as coming specifically from England. Another example is "they's," as in "They's trouble coming down the road," which is Scottish in origin and is an abbreviation or shortened version of "there is."

Once, I was visiting my mother, who lived in Bedford, Pennsylvania. I was outside a restaurant in the central part of the state on a cold winter's day when the lady who owned the place came out and kindly said to me, "You'in's c'mon in." I smiled, and, gently offended, she said, "Are you laughing at the way I talk?"

"No, ma'am," I replied. "We talk the same way where I come from three hundred miles southwest of here near the Great Smoky Mountains, in the Southern Appalachians." The use of the term "you-in's," Dr. Montgomery taught us, is Irish in origin. It's commonly used around East Tennessee today, and if you go to Dublin anytime soon, you can still hear people say, "Yousin's come see us!"

Other Irish traits are "big un" for "big one," "little un" for "little one," "his'n" for "his one" and "her'n" for "her one." Many Southern mountain terms are simply contractions of two or more other words, like "nairy one of them" for "neither one nor the other of them."

Herb Trentham from Baskin's Creek in the Great Smoky Mountains explained this to us once. His place of origin, near Gatlinburg, Herb's home community, was originally named Bear Skins Creek. But the name is lost forever due to an adaption by a National Park mapmaker during the early years of the National Park. "Bear Skins Creek" was altered to "Baskins" because the map-maker simply thought it was a good idea and that the new name was infinitely better than the old one. Whether this is true or not is irrelevant. The old, actual name is lost. "Baskins" is commonly used now and probably will be forever.

In any event, when Herb went to school, his teacher accused him of "learning English by a short-cut." Herb didn't understand his teacher and said to her, "Around my house, teacher, we don't say 'sit' and 'set' and 'sat.' We say nairy one of them."

"Well, Herb," the teacher at the Pi Phi School asked him, "At your house, how would you say it?"

"Well, at my house," young Herb Trentham said, "we just say 'sot.' It don't matter if'n we're gonna sot now or sot a while ago. It's still just sot!" Again, if Smoky Mountain speech is anything, it is practical.

Also, in Southern mountain speech, we adapt and make up words. Once, we were listening to Maynard Ledbetter of Townsend, Tennessee, talking about old John McCauley, who lived in Cades Cove. Mr. Ledbetter explained, "John McCauley was a great 'liver' in here." He wasn't referring to an internal organ, of course, but to the fine manner in which the man John McCauley lived.

Another time, I asked a man who was running a sawmill near the Big South Fork how he got his logs off the truck. In all seriousness, he said, "Why, I reckon, we just tumble-bugged them off a'there." We knew exactly what he meant, even though he was making up the word from two other descriptive words, which is a common East Tennessee language trait.

Linguists would say Southern mountain speech is inventive. We alter and make up words. From soda we get "sodi," from opera we get "opry," and from the "grand opera," we get the "grand ole opry." I'm not sure where the use of double nouns comes from. But again, it is descriptive and colorful, if nothing else. The words "long rifle" and "rifle-gun" are examples. However, it could be argued that the word "rifle" is simply describing the kind or type of barrel of a particular gun: a rifled barrel, thus, "rifle-gun."

"Tooth dentist" is perhaps descriptive to a fault of being repetitious. But it certainly leaves no doubt what the dentist's business is. The addition of "tooth" to "dentist" describes the actual work being done, probably for the customer's sake. Remember, prior to 1950 there were very few dentists in the Southern Appalachians. Teeth were usually pulled by barbers, hardware store clerks, feed-store operators and the like—anywhere a pair of pliers could be found.

Another interesting double-noun used particularly around East Tennessee is a baseball term, "hind catcher," and it's the only place I've ever heard it used. "Catcher" is sufficient information to know which baseball position we're talking about as far as most people are concerned. Adding "hind" to "catcher" certainly clarifies and describes exactly where on the baseball field the catcher plays. But the catcher can't play behind himself or herself, can they? The catcher is behind the batter. Yet again, "hind catcher" is descriptive to the point of repetition.

Numbers and the use of specifics are rarely part of Southern mountain speech. We once asked a man at Station Camp, a ford used to cross the Big South Fork River, "How many people were killed here?" We knew it was more than three.

He said, "Ah, they's several."

"How many, exactly?" I asked.

"Oh," he replied, "a right smart." Similar to those who frequently use "I reckon" or "maybe" to answer direct questions, the man from the Big South Fork wasn't being rude or particularly evasive. "Several" can mean two hundred. It comes from a time when people were in community, when my family might plow your ground and pick your corn if you got sick. Your uncles and brothers would come over and cut or thresh our wheat if we couldn't get to it. We did it together. Nobody kept a time clock. Everything was bartered and non-specific.

These tendencies to negotiate everything remain in our speech linguistically and come from this time of community. The linguists might say they remain with us today in the common use of "I reckon," "maybe," or "I don't care too" when used for "yes." An example might be if someone asks, "You want to go to town?" and the Southern mountain speaker says, "I don't care too." In Appalachia or the Ozarks it means yes, he will go. However, in most of the rest of the country, it means no, he doesn't want to go.

Our Love of R's

East Tennessee's love of the letter "r" is one of the most prevailing characteristics of Southern mountain speech. Dr. Montgomery says it's directly linked to our border Scots origins.

Charlotte Ross recognizes it, too. She says, "We no longer trill our 'r's' as when a Scot pronounces the name William Wallace. But nevertheless, we stick 'r's' in, every chance we get."

This raises the question, how many "r's" are in the East Tennessee use of the word "wash?" If it weren't written down, most would say four, because that's the way it sounds. To a Southern mountain speaker or listener, not inserting an "r" in "wash" just doesn't sound correct.

We no longer trill our "r's" the way Scotty from *Star Trek* does when he screams, "I cahn't doo it, cap'n. She woon't take it! I cahn't get choo any moor powrrrr!" But it's the same "r" sound we hear when we're told to "Go warsh the winders" or "Go get the minner bucket!" It's wonderful to recognize, finally, where

Maynard Ledbetter and mountain

this particular trait comes from, where it originates. It explains our penchant for the use of "r."

Likewise, for Maynard Ledbetter and his neighbors and friends, when they say, "Mr. McCauley was a great liver in here," it can only be interpreted one way: that he knew how to live. The fact that we, me or you and some other folks from California, perhaps, don't know what they are talking about or intend is irrelevant. They may think John McCauley's internal dark, gushy organ, the one that sits near the kidney and strains liquor and other toxicants from the blood, is somehow like John McCauley or something. That's not Maynard's concern. On the contrary, it is not even part or parcel of Maynard Ledbetter's worldview, or that of his neighbors. They know exactly what he's talking about.

I think this is what Dr. Cratis Williams means when he talks about mountain speech and its speakers having difficulty using words that require movement of the facial muscles and use of the back of the throat, like the long "e" sound and "ah," which requires the speaker to open his or her mouth like at the doctor's office – presuming the speaker was fortunate enough to visit a "sawbones."

The combination of the "a-in" verb is as common to our ears as cornbread. It is still being used by great numbers of people. One can recognize it when Wiley Oakley of the Great Smoky Mountains says, "I was just *a-waitin'* fer her to call me." Or "We were *a-gettin'* ready to go *a-singin'* and *a-sangin'*." This means we were getting ready to go into the mountains to sing and hunt the herb ginseng.

Charlotte Ross says that people of the Southern mountains have been *a-goin'* and *a-comin'*, *a-singin'* and *a-sangin'* since the days of Chaucer. Instinctively, we add the letter "a" sound to "ing" verbs. Again, it's used as an abbreviation of two words. Possibly, it is used for musical reasons, too, as it is more pleasing and allows the "ing" verb to roll, bounce, and move along lyrically, as does the music of a Southern mountaineer.

Arlenia West of Huntsville, Tennessee, does something lyrical like this when speaking about doing her chores when it rains. She says, "Wet days come, I wash n' iron and thangs." This is very simple, but profound, I think. She could say what she means, "When it rains, I wash and iron." Instead, she uses very few words to instinctively, intuitively speak in a lyrical manner. We know exactly what she means when she says "wet days come." Her use of alliteration instinctively creates a very poetic pleasing phrase that communicates clearly her intentions.

It is standard practice in society today to use "correct speech," whatever that is. Usually, it is the language that the majority of people use. What I mean to say is we speak in community; we talk like the people we look up to. In society, we speak like the powerful and elite. Language traits are normally those of society's wealthiest citizens. Language and the way we speak are socializing acts. Politics has more to do with speech than with breeding. It's about power rather than rules.

That's why, according to John Rice Irwin of the Museum of Appalachia, Appalachian people and the ways we talk in the Southern mountains are still ridiculed by the majority of the American academia and media. Speech is more about power than style. Mr. Irwin is correct when he says that Southern

Mann Ledbetter, Maynard's Pap, second from right, on hunting trip outside Cades Cove

mountain people, Appalachian people, are the last group of folks in America that it's still okay to make fun of.

For instance, when someone from Appalachia says, "There's a bar cum through here," people laugh, even though as many as six million people from Appalachia might speak this way. But people rarely laugh when someone from the Piedmont section of North Carolina says, "They-ea's a ba-eh in th' woods."

No one thinks anything about it, possibly because people in the Piedmont section of North Carolina who speak like this usually live in $400,000 homes, while the fellow who says "bar" may not. He may, in fact, live in a trailer and talk the same way

As a disenfranchised, lower socio-economic group, Appalachian folks hold less status. Therefore, they aren't setting the language standard for common speech, even though regionally their usage is widely spoken. They do not hold enough economic status to be imitated. Their language, this way of speaking, is unacceptable to the whole. It's ironic, because those mansion-owners in the Piedmont are considerably fewer in number but not in economic and political clout, which is typically the all-important socializing tool in society.

Many people will gladly purchase a 150-year-old antique and revere its quaint and authentic nature, its originality of style and personality. Yet, at the same time, they'll ridicule an old-timer whose "a-goin's" and "a-comin's" are familiar, but not really understood. However, this old-timer is using an authentic language that has been used for over 150 years. We respect and value material antiques, but not linguistic ones, even when one usage is more authentic in many ways than another. Often, it has been handed down for generations, though the speaker himself may not even be aware of it. Like the rest of us, he might think "It's just something old Grand-Pap might have said. He often talked that way or it might have just been something my father used to say."

Bill's Little Stories

Jesse Butcher said this happened in Maynardville, Tennessee, in Union County. An old farmer wearing bib overalls came in to the hardware store to buy an air conditioner. It was one hot July day, and the old man had his money in his chest pocket and was going to pay cash.

"Ah," the old man barked, scratching the back of his neck. "I need me an air conditioner!"

The kid behind the sales desk just got outta U.T. and thought he knew everything. Besides, he didn't think the old man was serious nor had any money. So, he says real snotty like, "How many BTU's you need, old timer?"

The old farmer looks at the kid and barks back, "I reckon enough to cool this B.U.T. The size of a T.U.B!"

Jesse, a National Heritage fellow, won $50 with this story in Washington D.C.

Old School Football

"You just got one pair of shoes for the season. One pair of shoes, that's all we had when we played football," he said to me.

I was at a gathering celebrating the full-color publication of the program for the upcoming Webb School's football season. Everyone at this event was excited about it. The magazine-style booklet was classy, with features and stats on each player and full color photographs. You didn't even have to be a senior. There was a picture and write-up of everybody on the team, including the managers. It was nice, fancy, and real snappy.

Senator Brenda Duncan Massey's campaign manager and I got to talking about what it was like when we played football almost forty years ago, sounding like a couple of old duffers. A lot sure has changed since then.

We realized this as soon as we began our conversation. It's really unbelievable the difference between then and now. Here it comes: we used to walk to school barefoot in snow up to our necks, up-hill both ways. Yeah, yeah. But it really was a lot different then. He played at Jellico High School, and I played for Notre Dame in Chattanooga in the late 1960s.

"We certainly didn't have anything like this program when we played football in high school, how about you?"

"We were lucky to have the name of our school spelled correctly. We never had our names on our shirts or our jerseys."

"I'm talking about spelling our names correctly on those one-page mimeographed, hand-out sheets."

"Ours was Xeroxed, I think. It was a one-page sheet listing everybody's name. It might have had our weight on that page, as well. Generally, it was within ten or twenty pounds of being correct."

"Yeah, and it still listed two or three people who had been

kicked off the team earlier in the season. And, maybe, two others who quit during two-a-day practices. Ha."

"I think they ran off copies once for the entire season and that was it. You were lucky if your parents got one sheet. If not, too bad."

"At Jellico High School, we just had twenty guys, twenty football players on the whole team. That's it—twenty players in four grades. Uniforms were hard to come by, too, at Jellico High School."

"You only got one pair of cleats. You had to take care of them. We loved those shoes, our cleats."

"One time, one of our guys got hurt during practice. I was across on the other side of the field when he got hurt; a defensive back broke his collarbone breaking up a pass. Everybody played both ways. Anyway, by the time I reached the coach, three other players had already gotten to him to ask if they could have his shoes! Everybody wanted his shoes. I sure did."

"You ever wonder about how they wouldn't ever let you get hurt?"

"I know what you mean."

"You weren't allowed to get hurt. They wouldn't let you get hurt, even if you did!"

"Except for knees injuries. People were always getting their knees blown out. We didn't have very good surgeries back then on the knees. If you hurt your knee you were pretty much done for the year anyway."

"Unless you got into the whirl pool. That was the miracle cure."

"At Notre Dame High School in Chattanooga, we had a coach and no matter what your ailment was, he'd tell you to get into the whirl pool. The whirly would fix anything. 'Coach, I've got something wrong with my hip.' 'Get into the whirly, son.' That's the way he put it. It was his cure for everything."

"Or, they might tell you to run on it, 'run it out.'"

"Yeah, most of the time, they thought it was just a bruise or a 'hammy.' Everything connected to your torso below your neck was your hamstring muscle! Ha! They never knew what was the matter with anybody anyway except for a pulled hammy!"

"One time we were playing a game and it was half-time. We

had a defensive back, Marti Arnold's older brother. I forget his first name. He was a good football player, too. He could hardly walk, much less run. I remember he hurt his leg pretty badly in the first half. At half-time, the coaches had him running up and down the sidelines trying to run it out."

"If you couldn't get into the whirley, you had to run it out, I guess. They thought if you ran far enough, magically your leg injury would just go away and you'd be all better!"

"Well, old Marti Arnold's brother was running up and down the sidelines trying to run it out, but he never could. He never did get back into that game."

"How bad was his injury?"

"He had a broken femur. That big leg bone was broken. Man. This happened where the AT&T Baseball Field is now in Chattanooga. It was the old Kirkman High School field, then. We were gathered behind the bleachers. There wasn't any place else for the visiting team to go. I can still see Arnold running up and down, limping, behind those bleachers. He was hurting, too. Ow!"

"I guess so. And we never had any water. During two-a-day practices at the beginning of the season when it is so hot, we never got any water to drink. Did you?"

"No, they didn't let us have any water; our coaches didn't, at least not at that time."

"They thought water was bad for you or something."

"Or, it would make you weak or something, or turn you into a girl. Instead, they just gave you salt tablets. They did us. We'd get dozens of them, big handfuls of salt tablets. We'd take twelve to fifteen before each practice, sometimes twice a day."

"A lot of guys would puke them up, too. They actually would sometimes. But they never would give us any water. Yeah, that whole water thing was crazy."

"But we did get water during games. Did you?"

"We didn't have water girls or water boys or anything like that. We just had a towel."

"A towel?"

"Yeah, a towel and a bucket. It was pretty goofy. If there was a time out, or between quarters or something, they would bring it in, just bring us a towel. It was a wet towel kept in a bucket of water. They would just bring the towel, though. They wouldn't bring the bucket. This only went on for about half the season. We'd be in the huddle or something during a time-out. Then, we'd hear somebody say, 'Thank God, here comes some water.' The manager would run out onto the field carrying a big wet towel. The bottom of it would be dragging the ground picking up all kinds of stuff, little bits of white chalk and dirt. But that didn't matter.

"The first guy to get the towel was usually a big lineman, a tackle, or somebody. First thing he'd do is wipe the sweat, dirt, and grime off of his face; then he'd grab the towel and take a big suck. He'd suck it. That's how we got our water. We'd suck it from the towel.

"The next guy would wipe the snot and blood off his face and then he'd suck the towel; a different part of the towel, if he could. You always tried to find a clean place on the towel to get your drink. You didn't want to be the last guy to get the towel and try to get your drink. Pretty funny, thinking about it now. It was crazy, huh?

"When the towel came out, the crowd always moaned, 'Ooow!' You could hear them collectively groan when the first guy started sucking on the towel. Some doctors and other folks raised so much hell about it, saying it was filthy and nasty, that they finally put an end to it. I guess it was the only way the coaches could figure out how to get water to the troops."

"I guess."

"Then, finally, late in the season, somebody brought out a plastic bucket with some kind of a ladle or a big spoon, and we each got a little bit of water. I guess that was progress."

"Yeah," my new friend said, "those were the good old days."

An Olympic Memory

Every athlete, parent, and coach understands you get out of a sport what you put into it. Isn't that what our old coaches used to say?

The beauty of the Olympics and why we love them is because to win you have to put your heart and soul into it. It's an equation, not a gift. That's why we love our local champions—Dee Dee Trotter, Davis Tarwater, Justin Gatlin, Tianna Madison, Aries Merritt, Candace Parker, Tamika Catchings, and Claire Donahue, our girl from Lenoir City. Even though we don't know them, we still love them for what they've achieved. We admire their discipline and sacrifice.

Forty years ago, another relay team won the Georgia State Swimming Championships for boys aged 15–17. You don't know them and never will. But I was lucky enough to be their coach, and I'll never forget that day. If you knew Frank, Jimmy, Allen, and Billy, you'd love them, too. They overcame adversity, like all championship athletes.

They're all our children, aren't they? We see them that way. That's why we ache when our athletes falter, tremble, and fail, just like us. We get knocked down every day. We fail, we're scared, and we don't live up to our potential. But champions do, and we love them for it. They fail, too, but somehow they get up, dust themselves off, and continue striving for greatness. In so doing, they improve their PBs, or personal bests, as they call them. For athletes, it's the Holy Grail. You can't always win, but achieving a PB is a requirement to be a champion.

The boys I coached weren't so different from thousands of other teenagers except they kept coming to practice, trying to improve, all summer long. I can still see their carefree sixteen-year-old smiling faces—unless they were swimming sprints! Then, they fussed, probably like US Olympic swimmers Missy

Franklin, Rebecca Soni, Dana Vollmer, and Allison Schmitt, even though their coach calls them the Smiley Gang.

Allen, Billy, Jimmy, and Frank didn't compete against Australia or China but swam against DeKalb County and greater Atlanta, a team made up of all-stars. In preparing them for their relay finals, all I could do was put them in the right order. Billy played football, was sturdy, dependable, and gave you everything. Allen was slight, thin, and never gave up. Cocky Jimmy was fun loving, but not quite as good as he thought. Big Frank was legendary—a strong, gifted swimmer whose presence gave others faith in themselves.

For the finals, Jimmy stood tall, grinning on those starting blocks and feeling no pressure. There's something miraculous in the smiling innocence of young athletes. When they win, we feel it, too. With them it's pure joy! Happiness, satisfaction, accomplishment; it comes from working toward something and achieving it. As parents, coaches, and friends, we share it with them. We know the price they had to pay. We couldn't do it. But they did.

Jimmy stayed even. It was all we could ask of him. Allen fought hard, but lost two strokes. Billy picked up a body length, and Frank took off against the fastest swimmer in the state, winner of the individual fifty-yard freestyle race. Frank caught him at the wall but messed up his turn. Then, amazingly, he caught the guy again coming back! It was a photo finish! It took twenty minutes before they awarded our boys, these men, the gold medal. They earned it. You always do.

You have to earn it. It's just the way it is—what it takes to be a champion. But you'll never regret it. Not for a minute, ever.

The Harlequin Massacre

During the racially charged summer of 1971, I was a member of an acting troupe in Chattanooga, where it was our privilege to bring children's theater to underprivileged children. As part of the University of Tennessee at Chattanooga's Drama Department summer theater project, we performed a children's play entitled *The Sorcerer's Apprentice*. It was complete with evil frogs, pirates, bird witches and the like, and about as subversive or threatening as *The Cat in the Hat Comes Back*. Our second production was equally childlike; a story about a goofy pair of country bumpkins who stumble into court dreaming of becoming knights and fall under the influence of an evil prime minister who wants to be king.

The plays weren't controversial at all. There was nothing remotely political or racial about any of it, except we were white college students doing children's plays in predominately black areas. Amazingly, these performances culminated one hot summer's evening into a full-blown race riot! Personally, I'm not even sure what ignited it, other than we were simply in the wrong place at the wrong time.

Our theatrical troupe didn't offer much spirited resistance to almost fifty angry black folks. Being theater artists, we thought we were going to die. For that reason, we've always referred to the incident as a massacre rather than a riot because that's what it was.

All the men in the troupe and a few women were hospitalized, some at Erlanger, some at Memorial Hospital, after they were savagely beaten by forty-four young black men and women. John Gehring, who portrayed the young prince in the play, was

---

See color photographs of the Harlequin's performances (Plates 1-16).

beaten repeatedly with a baseball bat while sitting in a parked car. He and three others were waiting for the driver, Dennis Haskins, or for Jim Steele, who had the car keys. But Dennis was so badly beaten he couldn't make it back to the car. The car was nearly totaled with the four people inside. My little brother was hit in the head with a lead pipe, which fractured his skull. He was about fifteen years old at the time.

From this event sprang a myriad of court cases. Many of the riot participants were in fact brought to trial, but the trials dragged on for months. Initially, many brave first-hand witnesses came forward and testified. However, as the case dragged on and on, fewer witnesses returned. Ultimately, only two huge black men were left as eyewitnesses, along with our troupe, a few white witnesses, and our teachers. In spite of many physical threats, these brave men stood their ground as the sole black witnesses against the rioters. As a result, two black men were found guilty and convicted of inciting the riot.

Documenting History

Forty years after this pivotal eruption in the staid storyline of our lives, this event deserves a fresh look – if for no other reason than it has never before been completely told to the public.

To say this group of students and teachers were enormously affected by the bizarre series of events is an understatement. Of course we were – both physically and mentally. How much? We've no idea, but we would like to find out.

It is my hope that, through the retelling of this story and additional research, somehow we might find out. It would be interesting, but it would also be helpful to know how this event affected the lives of the dozens of young and old black people present at the riot, as well as the white audience members and teachers. They had to have been affected. Did viewing this alter their lives in any way? What about the impact on the forty-four accused attackers? Did it solidify or disturb their way of thinking and living? What about those who were convicted; what do they think and feel about all of this, today?

Prologue to the Harlequins

Our director, Dorothy Hackett Ward, named our theatrical troupe the Harlequins. Though this name reflected our Elizabethan style of production, as an improvisational troupe, we saw ourselves more like Chicago's 2nd City Players or other guerilla theater groups then plying their trade in late 1960s America. The word "harlequin" was just a little too fey for our tastes. But ours was not a democratic unit. It was a directorship, and Dorothy Hackett Ward was the director. There was never any doubt or discussion about it.

A fearless, tireless, Yale Drama school educated, gifted teacher, director, and diva, Mrs. Ward was the greatest teacher most of us ever saw. We were fortunate to be able to say that our formative college years were under her tutelage. This in itself opened many doors, near and far, throughout our lives. We were better artists and human beings because of her. We were year-round students, and it was not easy.

For two successive summers, we rehearsed and performed every day from 5:30 in the afternoon until 10:00 pm. The first year, the summer of 1970, was tremendously difficult. After whatever summer jobs we college kids could cobble together, each of us dragged our sorry, tired selves down to the UTC theater building and rehearsed, day after day, night after night. But we loved it.

There, at the Theater Center, we portrayed the great kings of our imaginations. We concocted and created queens, heroes and heroines, and tragic love stories. We created epic tales, fables, and faerie stories involving Theseus and the Minotaur, Humpty Dumpty, and other real and mythological characters from literature or the imaginations and mechanizations of Dorothy and Jim Lewis, our technical director, great friend, and supporter.

Together, they taught us everything they could about everything they could. It included, but was not limited to, the theater. Whatever they knew—and they knew a great deal—was transferred and infused into us. We were like sponges ready to soak it up. Together, as students, players, and a group, we were hungry and desperate in our energy and quest to add meaning to our lives. Dorothy Hackett Ward and Jim Lewis showed us where and how to find it, then presented it to us on a platter in the theater.

They handled us almost as "good cop, bad cop," as far as our theatrical training was concerned. Mrs. Ward, often tyrannical and impulsive, was passionately creative in flurries, with the energy of a thirty year old, while Jim Lewis was always understanding and supportive. Dorothy was as old as Methuselah; Jim was maybe ten years older than we were. We believed Mr. Lewis understood us better. He sought to make our jobs and lives easier, while Mrs. Ward worked us like rented mules. Occasionally, they switched roles and responsibilities.

Improvisational theater afforded us the creative freedom to express the topical and emotional concerns of our times. We were able to do this even when our choice of plays, subjects, and characters did not. For instance, when Jimi Hendrix died in September 1970, we dedicated the entire performance that night in his honor. Some of us even wore black armbands. Thinking back on it now, we were genuinely saddened and grief stricken. We performed that night in Bell Buckle, Tennessee. In recalling that illustrious event, we weren't exactly sure who comprised our particular audience that evening, or that they even knew what a Jimi Hendrix was, or cared! But we did. It was real enough to us, and that's what counted—likewise when Janis Joplin died.

Martin Luther King had recently been slain in 1968, and Bobby Kennedy shortly afterwards. John Kennedy had already been assassinated too, of course. The streets were afire with the energy of a tumultuous time. The radical, fiery sixties had given way to a new decade, and it wasn't starting off too well. It seemed full of ominous, dark shadows and very near the end of hope. There were killings and death where once there was energy and light. Meanwhile, by the Harlequin Players' second summer, the entire City of Chattanooga had become increasingly more contentious, heated, untrusting, and angry. In the midst of all this, here we were, lucky us. Fifteen young struggling theater artists trying to learn, have some fun, and make a difference—like most everyone else in our generation.

The 1960s and 70s

By 1971, there had occurred at least two very public, racially mo-
tivated hate crimes in Chattanooga. In addition, nearby, there
was some resurgent Klu Klux Klan activity along the Georgia
and Alabama borders, not far from the city. We periodically
lived under a curfew.

The National Guard had been called out five-thousand strong
to quell a disturbance following a Wilson Pickett concert at the
Memorial Auditorium on McCallie Avenue. It happened one
Saturday night when the promoters refused to pay the black artists in advance of their concert. In response, they simply refused
to go on stage. The mostly black audience, who had already paid
for their tickets, was incensed. They went berserk, raged, and
rioted, throwing garbage cans through windows as they stormed
outside and took to the streets, overturning a police car or two
in the process.

Another episode involved a very public criminal court case
related to an attempted murder. The convicted criminal had received a lesser sentence for the crime than many of the city's
black citizens thought appropriate. They were outraged. Many
of the black leaders said they'd had about enough. There had
already been one black man murdered, and many thought this
was the last straw. Though it's dramatic to say that Chattanooga
was a tinderbox ready to explode, this was pretty much the case.
It was a very dangerous, volatile situation.

Any small disturbance at any time could erupt into crisis.
America was confronting a new age of separate but unequal
races, and Chattanooga in 1971 was a delicate minefield of racial animosity. And it was building, growing worse not better.
Anyone who was alive then will remember the pervasive, eerie,
unsettling feeling on the streets of not trusting anybody.

Whether anyone knew it or cared, we, the Harlequin bunch,
were on the black's side of most racial issues of the day. Through
our plays like *The Sorcerer's Apprentice,* which depicted epic country bumpkins, evil prime ministers, and dangerous mysterious
frogs, we brought smiles, laughter, and squeals of joy to the hot
streets and the children of Chattanooga, both black and white,
during the summers of 1970 and 1971.

Of course, we worked the first year without any pay. But during our second year, a grant helped fund our operations. It resulted in better equipment and a vehicle. Prior to getting the truck, most of us just piled in with the few who had cars and drove to wherever the performance was scheduled. The grant also afforded us a small stipend. "Hey, we became actual working actors," we might have said, though we all certainly kept our day jobs. Rather, most of us did.

Robert Duffy and Larry Von Wersowetz, the technical wizards among us, worked full time for the theater (and did not quit for the rest of their lives!). They concocted our magic cauldrons and built the collapsible stages that could be mounted and struck in accordance with the City Parks and Recreation truck schedule. It was the beginning of our careers in entertainment and theater, which many of us enjoyed for the rest of our lives.

Our single rental truck followed along or met the City Parks and Recreation Department's big eighteen-wheeler, which contained the stage we used. It also carried other equipment such as Ping–Pong tables, books, board games, and other recreational toys.

Our vehicle carried our theater props, trunks, and costumes for the two different shows we did, as well as stage auxiliary pieces. We had the truck rigged with two loud speakers. When we arrived, the world knew it. As we drove up, we turned up the sound and threw away the knob. Tchaikovsky's *1812 Overture* boomed and blared via the speakers Larry had mounted to the truck's mirrors. Everywhere we performed that summer, across many of Chattanooga's poorest neighborhoods, the *1812 Overture* announced the coming of joy, entertainment, and laughter with the arrival of the Harlequin Players!

We performed on dead-end streets and in open fields. As soon as we arrived, the women of the troupe went to work. Bo Robinson, Ellen Lynsky, Arlene Ruttenburg, Lynn Narramore, and the sisters Carol and Susan Miles put on their clown costumes and rounded up our audience. It was the clown costumes that did it. As soon as the children saw them, they instantly knew no fear. The very appearance of clowns brought out the children by the hundreds – carefully at first, then with fearlessness and wonder. They came to see the show!

Harlequins in Performance

Plate 1. Show begins with Harlequin introduction

Plate 2. Apprentice with witches and children

Plate 3. View of typical Chattanooga show

Plate 4. Children enjoying a performance

Plate 5. Children watching birds on stage

Plate 6. Wide shot showing Park equipment in use

Plate 7. School yard becomes a theater in no time,
as Apprentice performs with children

Plate 8. Neighborhood-wide frog attack, side shot

Plate 9. Large crowd with Robert Duffy by stage

Plate 10. Wide view of set, truck, and audience as Bo Robinson waits in the wings

Plate 11. Frog jumping at the audience

Plate 12. Lenny Gaddis as the Apprentice with a Pirate who looks like me

Plate 13. Sad good witch

Plate 14. Boys enjoying the show

Plate 15. Smiling boys in audience

Plate 16. Little girls on front row

The Tomato Wars

Plate 17

Pirate Paddy O'Dea

Plate 18

In empty parking lots, playgrounds, wherever the City Parks and Recreation vehicles were already set up and chose to spend the day, we joined them to perform every day all summer at 4:30 or 5:00 p.m. It was always hot, most days way over ninety degrees. While the women rounded up the audience, Duffy, Larry Von, Mac, Kirby Moore, Dennis Haskins, Jim Steele, Jerry Satterfield, John Gerhing, John David Curry, and I busied ourselves unloading props and setting up.

The truck was behind the set, arranged at a ninety-degree angle to the stage like a "T." The back of the truck opened up, and we pulled the stage floor out and set it up. The audience, of course, couldn't see the truck. All they could see was the backdrop, the amazing, huge, painted medieval scene and set. It was made up of half-a-dozen or more connected painted flats. When assembled, it was approximately fifteen-feet high and twenty-five-feet long. It was huge. Each panel stood nearly ten-feet tall and gave the appearance of a twenty-foot backdrop behind a very usable six-foot stage area. The stage was four feet off the ground, so the audience could see everything (see Plates 1, 7, and 10).

We presented our plays in the round with four different performing areas. One was directly opposite the main stage area with two smaller areas on either side. It was a little like a baseball diamond where each base was a place to perform with the audience all around.

The children usually sat in the middle directly in front of the main stage. We had one-hundred children at performances, sometimes as many as two-hundred. Their ages ranged from nursing babies to two year olds to fourteen- or fifteen-year-old teenagers and, of course, the adults.

It became clear from the beginning that we needed to involve the children in the performances, and we did. We learned quickly that we actually needed to talk directly to the audience, and damn if they wouldn't talk back to you in response. They always answered anything that sounded like a question to them.

If we looked at the audience and said, "Oh, no, what am I going to do now?" we had to be ready for an answer, because they were going to tell us. We had no idea what they were going to say either, like, "Oh, no, you goofy prince, don't pull nothing out of that book of recipes!" Or, "Don't be messin' with those magic potions. Somethin' BAD is gonna happen!"

Sure enough, they were right, too. The audience always screamed when big green frogs came up out of the cauldron (see Plate 11). "I told you not to mess with that MAGIC!" someone would holler out. Or, "No, no, no, don't you be pickin' that up," or "Yeah, yes sir! You right, that's the way!" Or, "Oh, no! Don't be doin' that! You dummy!" But we did it anyway, much to the delight of everybody.

Once, at least, during every performance, the King would ask for the audience to help against the evil Prime Minister. Usually, at this point, their antics were hilarious. By this time, the Prime Minister is hiding the country bumpkins behind his cape, dancing around, and trying to hide them from the King. As this is going on, Jim Steele, as the King, stands up seriously and asks Duffy, "What's the matter with you, Prime Minister, what are you doing? What's going on there, what's ailing you?"

Duffy keeps dancing and dodging, trying to hide his accomplices while continuing his goofy jig. He says, "Ah, it's just an old war wound, Sire!" When he does, the King picks up on it too and starts to join the Prime Minister as both dance around, grabbing their legs, with the bumpkins still hiding behind the Prime Minister's cape.

The King, still dancing around, says happily, "WELL, Prime Minister, I guess it's nothing a few days in Florida won't cure, Eh?!" I remember lines like these delighted everyone, even all the skeptical adults and older teenagers who were the hardest to win over to the fun of live theater.

With this kind of zaniness going on, the audience always felt compelled to join in. It was fun. They would give directions, anything any of us needed, any kind of help to make the show work out. There wasn't any third or fourth wall in these productions. The audience participated wholeheartedly as characters. You never knew what they were going to do or what they were going to say. As actors, we had to be ready.

Just as the audience and the players worked together, the park operations had to work closely with the theatrical side. There could be no disharmony. The City Parks and Recreation Department programs were overseen by Coach Henry Bowles, who was the head coach of the Howard Hustlin' Tigers basketball program for years. He managed the parks and recreation operations onsite.

Coach Bowles's predominately black athletic teams at Howard High School were tremendously successful in those years. In 1967, for instance, Notre Dame High, where I went to school, played Howard in football. They were ranked second in the state, and they beat us 56–0. It was embarrassing. I lost thirteen pounds that night chasing their players all over the football field. We never beat them in basketball.

Coach Bowles ran the recreation department, and Mrs. Dorothy Hackett Ward was in charge of the theatrical operations. Everyone worked well together. We were an all-white theatrical troupe, but the parks department employees would help us set up, even occasionally portraying a minor character or two. They didn't rehearse with us, though. We did that back at the theater. They did their thing, and we did ours. We all got along, had our different responsibilities and interests, and performed them well.

Trouble at Alton Park

The play we presented this particular summer night was a typical production. There wasn't anything controversial about it. It wasn't *Uncle Tom's Cabin,* a monologue involving Malcolm X, or anything like that.

It was a children's play about two country bumpkins coming to the court to become knights. At the court of the King, they're used and misused by the evil Prime Minister, portrayed by Robert Duffy, who sees his chance to manipulate the two knuckleheads to his advantage against the King by a series of shenanigans. The King was portrayed ingeniously by a skinny, long-black-haired actor, Jim Steele, who was certainly one of the most talented and gifted performers amongst us.

Mac Smotherman, who later became the chairman of the UTC theater department, played one of the country bumpkins, and I played the other. The play was about as sophisticated as *Rumplestiltskin,* or any of *Grimm's Fairy Tales.* It didn't matter; the audience loved it. The climactic scene featured a medieval jousting tournament, complete with at least two competing horses that Larry Von created by welding together rebar and steel and putting leather straps on them. These imaginary horses could run, using the actor's hooves, of course. It was pretty amazing stuff for the time, and certainly theatrical.

These plays were improvised, so we, as actors, often made up lines and actions, much to the pleasure of the children. In my mind, I often picture the women and girls of our troupe, especially Lynn Narramore, who is no longer with us. She always portrayed Raggedy-Ann complete with a bright red-haired wig in pigtails. Most of the women wore big red clown noses and rounded up the children each night as the Pied Piper of Hamlin did, while music blared from the loud speakers.

All of this had been rehearsed, of course. We'd probably performed the same play more than forty times already during the summer. We could do either of two different productions anytime. This night we were doing our second show, which was the one that ended with a jousting match.

Previously, we had performed *The Sorcerer's Apprentice,* a production where green frogs appear out of a steaming cauldron. Then, the frogs turn and approach the audience, actually climbing out of the cauldron! It was great. Until the last moment, the frogs are hidden from view. The actors, and there were always three frogs, would crawl under the stage through a little hole, a trap door in the back of the cauldron. The frogs were all wrapped up in a gauze-like, green costume material. When they first stuck their green heads out of that witches pot, everyone went crazy! And, when those frogs crawled out of that cauldron toward the screaming children, it was always bedlam. Fred Park, we all agreed, was the greatest frog king to ever crawl from a cauldron, but he wasn't able to join us for this our second season. I'll remember those frogs as long as I live!

I have to say that in my life I have been on many athletic teams, including championship swimming teams. But in every one of those different team sports, I can't remember all of the names of my teammates. This is not the case with that troupe of actors, some of my longest and dearest friends, the Harlequin Players. Even after forty years, I can remember each and every member, every one of them as if they were a member of my family. I'm sure it's because of what we all experienced together, especially that evening. "We few, we happy few, we band of brothers . . ."

The particular show that evening was held at Spencer Mc-Callie Homes in Alton Park. It's an area located on the east side, not far from Howard High School, and a few miles from the foot of Lookout Mountain, not too far from what is called St. Elmo. Spencer McCallie Homes is a large housing complex arranged by square streets. It's what's commonly called "the projects," with similar houses/apartments all arranged and lined up together for blocks and blocks. It is organized like a large maze. Upon entering, you keep going and going deeper and deeper inside until you finally reach the cheese in the center.

In our case, the cheese was a community playground complex tucked deep inside at the center of what seemed like an endless complex of army barracks. At its center were basketball courts, a parking area, and an open playing field where the performance was to be held (see Plates 6 and 9).

Though we had been in project areas all that summer, this felt different. In the black and white cosmic world in which we existed then, it was as if we weren't supposed to be there, yet we were. Perhaps we shouldn't have been. But there was nothing we could do about it except to play our parts.

It was our fate. Though we didn't know anything was out of the ordinary at the time, it was. Looking back on it now, we should have left. We were told to go, and we should have. Instead, we were somewhere in a crowded place, yet isolated, a very long way from our white world and with no way of getting out. We were trapped in there, which is why it took the police so long to come and help us, if they ever did.

But there's one more thing: we *wanted* to be there. It was our mission that summer. It's where we could do the most good, and we believed that we were *supposed* to be there. It's what the grant was for; it's what we did.

I remember distinctly the show, the set-up that night. Things did not go well from the start. Something was wrong. What it was, and how wrong it actually turned out to be, no one yet knew.

I recall climbing into the back of our big rental truck, which served as the men's dressing room. To get in you simply pulled a curtain aside and entered. This is where we stored stuff, assembled after our specific set-up jobs were done, and changed into our costumes.

It was show time! It was time to "go on" and to put on our costumes and make-up, if we wore any. Our set-up jobs, half our night's work, were done. Now, we joined the gang for some fun, we thought. The rest of the night was always a joy, acting and performing. Even at twenty years old, it's what we lived for!

Inside the truck I had my first inkling of trouble. For some reason, one of the black employees of the Parks and Recreation Department staff was agitated. Though he didn't perform with us, he was a friend, like everyone there who worked for the Parks Department. After all, we saw him every day. But, unlike other nights, he seemed concerned. Something was very wrong.

Our young friend was telling Larry Von and others, including Mac Smotherman, that we had better leave! "Listen to me," he said. "You-all better do as they say and get out of here!" He wasn't kidding around.

This was our first hint of trouble, the first I knew anything was wrong. He was adamant. "They're not fooling around!" He continued, "If they told your director to leave, then, LEAVE! They mean it."

This was the first I'd heard anything of it. There had been some kind of confrontation. I'd walked into the middle of a discussion about it. It was all vague, though. There was some kind of Black Panther Party meeting that night at the Alton Park homes. It just happened that that group, or something akin to it, was there that night, and they didn't like us being there also. They didn't want us to do our show. A representative or representatives of the group had already approached Mrs. Ward or somebody from our group and had warned us that they didn't want us there.

Mrs. Ward or Mr. Lewis or both of them consulted with Coach Henry Bowles who assured them that he knew the majority of these young men and women, and these were "good kids." Everything was going to be fine, they were told. And that's what we were told, too.

Many of us didn't know there had been any warning or confrontation. All we knew was what our Parks Department friend told us. We had been warned to go, and we hadn't yet. He assured us again and again we should listen to what they were saying and leave. He was telling us this for our own good, and we believed him.

"Fine," we said. "We hear what you're saying! Goodbye!"

We jumped out of the truck and went to check with Mr. Lewis or Mrs. Ward. It seems like we found Mrs. Ward, related to her what our friend was saying, and suggested we should listen to what these people where telling us: they didn't want us here. Heck, we thought, a lot of other people and places do want us. Let's go there! We didn't know what was going on, but something wasn't right. We tried to explain this to Mrs. Ward or Coach Bowles. I can't remember whom we talked with about it. Mr. Lewis might have been there, too, but I can't remember.

Regardless, "no" was the word we got in response. We were not going to leave. There was an enormous crowd gathering. Already there were two or three-hundred children running around, settling in, and sitting down. It was decided we weren't going to leave. We were going to do this show.

How this discussion took place and where it happened I don't know. I just remember there was some dissention on our side about it. We disagreed and said as much. We wanted to leave; we argued our point. We believed our friend, and we told our superiors about it. But we were told to go ahead and do the show. "The show must go on" or something like it, although that wasn't exactly said. We were assured everything was going to be all right. Very soon after that, the play began.

The next thing I recall is the Prime Minister, Duffy, on the stage doing his soliloquy. Things were underway, but weren't going very well. Everybody seemed very tentative, like we were waiting. For what no one knew, but we felt that something was going to happen. Duffy held up a shiny coin of the realm and talked about having his face imprinted on all the money. He went on and on about his plan to take charge of the kingdom.

That was our cue. It was time for Mac and me to make our entrances from stage right; where we came around the backdrops talking and climbed the stairs onto the stage. Then, I remember two images. First, I peeked around from behind the flat, as I usually did, to get a quick look at the size and type of audience. Mac and I could see the audience was huge. Wow, there were perhaps two-hundred-fifty to three-hundred children. They were sitting everywhere. Some were standing with the adults, who were laughing at Duffy from behind their children. I was amazed. But something still didn't seem right. There was bad karma all around.

Then, suddenly I saw them coming. That is the second image. I saw a huge crowd coming from atop a hill to the side. It was a different kind of crowd, more like a mob. They were marching together almost in step, four abreast, and heading straight toward the show and us.

The audience was in front of them looking at the stage and didn't see them yet. I remember thinking, "They aren't the audience; they aren't coming to see the show. They're angry. They're coming for some other reason. Why are they angry? Where are they going? What's going to happen?"

It was a huge crowd of adults, maybe fifty, mostly angry black men and some women, too. They were dressed almost entirely in black and marching together like an army, coming straight for the stage.

It didn't add up, so I pulled back and waited for Duffy to give us our cue to enter. All I know is I came around the flat and was surprised and confused by all those adults, those marching black men and women I'd just seen farther up the hill. Now, so quickly, here they were right up against the front of the stage. They were standing right in front of the children. "Hey," I thought, "the children can't see! This isn't right; this isn't the way it's supposed to be."

Duffy, of course, was always great. He was portraying the evil Prime Minister with his usual flourish, in that flowing black cape, a.k.a. professor's cloak. It looked like a graduation robe. When suddenly, Duffy was pulled into the crowd and wasn't on stage any more. He was above the crowd. Was he flying? No, he was being roughly handled above the crowd, like at a Rave concert when a musician dives into the mosh pit. Except Duffy didn't jump; he was pulled, yanked by the cape into the crowd and disappeared. Then, all hell broke loose.

Something or someone rushed by me. Two or three black men passed by me on either side. I could see their angry faces. I can still see them. They grabbed the ten-foot flat and broke it in half. I was thinking, "Why are they doing that?" But everything was happening so fast, none of it registered. Wham! All of a sudden, I think I was hit in the face by a two-by-four! It felt like a board, a big piece of wood, hitting me right between the eyes.

A great pain sheered across my smashed face. My eyes watered immediately. I couldn't see. I went down to one knee. I grabbed for my face and felt my lip sliced and bleeding. I might have been hit with a fist, but whatever it was it had a tremendous force behind it. I was wavering, almost unconscious. I remember thinking to myself, "Don't get knocked down! Don't let them get you down off your feet, or you'll never get up. You'll be killed! Don't get knocked down! Stay up!"

I was being hit from all sides, particularly from the back. Lots of people were hitting me. These were fists, now, I'm sure of it, hitting me again and again – my ears, the back of my head, my side – blow after blow. Some of the blows were connecting, but weren't very hard, not like the first blow that cold-cocked me! I was moving now. I remember instinctively telling myself to move, to fight back!

Turning, I saw in front of me maybe five or seven of them, I don't know how many. I lunged and grabbed a head behind the neck with my left hand. As I did, I came over the top with my right hand. Pow! I hit back, and it felt good, too! Right on somebody's head, hard as I could. Then, again, they overwhelmed me. I fought back, moved, and didn't get knocked down. I grabbed another head. No hair, nearly bald. Wham! I hit it again. Then, they beat me again. "Ow, I think my hand's broken!" But I was finally free!

Suddenly, breathing hard like an animal, leaning against the back of the pick-up truck, I found myself panting, trying to get my wits back for a second. What the hell was going on? What was happening? I tried to focus. I was dizzy. I wiped blood from my face and mouth. My eyes were clearing a little, but my hand hurt, my face hurt, my back hurt.

Then, leaning against the truck, I saw the chaos. It was horrible! People running, screaming, but I couldn't hear any sounds. Look! They're tearing the set down! The set is coming down, children are crying. Oh God!

Suddenly, I could see a staggering Robert Duffy with a man or two swinging at him, grabbing his cape. He still wore that dumb black, swirling cape. They pulled at it to get to him. He couldn't move well, damn cape. But, that wasn't it—he was groggy, addled, as if playing drunk. But it was from being beaten. He was still being hit.

Robert staggered over between the pick-up truck and the trailer hitch, which he stepped over and then fell down. A black man who had been trying to get to Duffy picked up our big tool-box. It was made of heavy lumber and contained metal clamps, hammers, and heavy tools. He threw it down on Duffy's head and I thought, "Oh my God! That could kill him!"

They left me alone for a minute and finally quit beating me. I tried to get my wits about me. Then, I saw Jim Steele, all skinny 135 pounds of him on his six-foot frame, twenty feet away, maybe. He was unconscious. Five or six men, maybe in their twenties, were ruthlessly, maniacally kicking him in the face and the back of the head, again and again and again. He was already out cold, I thought. I could see his face, as his head was jerked, whipped around by the blows. His eyes were closed, thank God. Maybe, he couldn't feel anything. He wasn't fighting back—he couldn't. He didn't know how. He was on his hands and knees now, trying to crawl. "Whack!" His head jerked back towards me and blood flew out of his mouth. I saw him kicked in the head at least three times.

I still see this image in my head often, every time I think of this event. It used to be all the time. For years, when I think of this night, I see Jim's head, his long hair flicking, his eyes shut, being jerked by the blows; the boots, blood spitting from his mouth like spurting drool—with five or six vicious people raging at him, trying to hurt him as badly as they could, trying to kill him, erase his life. Why? Hate! Where is it coming from? Why? This was Jim Steele. I wanted them to know he wouldn't hurt a fly.

I remember grabbing the trumpet and running towards him—that dumb trumpet that calls the kingdom to order before the jousting tournament. I thought I could protect Jim, beat them off with that stupid long, brass trumpet. It could be a weapon, I thought. But, after two steps, I stopped short. They quit kicking Jim, and he lay still. I thought, "There's too many of them, they'll take this trumpet and wrap it around my head, or beat me with it, or stick it up my ass!" I was ashamed of myself for not going after them. I thought better of it. I threw the trumpet back into the bed of the truck.

I tried to pick Duffy up off the ground, but he was so heavy. Somehow, I saw Jim Lewis. He was being chased by two or three men. He started up across a little ravine or drainage ditch. Jim played basketball. He was six-foot-two-inches tall and weighed two-hundred pounds, a good-sized, big man. He went to Baylor University. I could see one of his attackers waving a big bottle as a weapon. It was heavy. The guy raised that Double Cola bottle fast and hit Jim Lewis right across the back of the skull—as hard as he possibly could. It hit him solidly in the back of the head. Immediately, Jim stumbled and fell down, blood spurting out the back of his neck.

The next thing I remember, I was in a car watching the mayhem everywhere through the window. The car was moving. I was looking out the back right window. It looked like a bomb had exploded in a big playground. There was smoke, screaming children running, and gravel flying. We were moving forward fast. I turned to look inside the car. Jim Lewis was driving. I could see the back of his neck and the opened gash at the base of his skull. There was blood everywhere. The wound was open but not bleeding so much anymore. I could see the pink meat of his flesh.

Imogene, his wife, was next to him. She was in shock, but aware of everything and helping to get us out of there: riveted, looking all around, first to the right, and then to the left, fast. Then, left to right and back again. It was like her head was on a swivel, jerking first one way then the other. She was watching out, intensely hoping the car wasn't running over anybody. She was also looking to help and pick up people. We had no idea if we were the first or last ones out. There was no way of knowing. We were on our own.

Jim's wheels were screeching. He was driving around in a

field or a playground/parking lot, picking up people, rescuing them. It was crazy! He told me later he fought the impulse to run over people! He was lucky to be awake. He had a concussion and couldn't see straight. He couldn't read for three months. I don't know how he could drive.

Suddenly, I remembered my brother, Paul! Where was he? I had to find him, I thought. I was okay in the back seat of Jim Lewis's car. Jim's wife, Imogene, was in the front passenger seat. Someone else was in the other back seat, I don't know who, maybe Jim Steele. Dennis? I don't know. "I can't leave my brother, Jim," I said. "Try to find Paul—let's find Paul. I've got to find my brother!" I remember that was the most horrible thing of all, leaving my brother there. Not knowing what had happened to him.

We finally got out of there. The car reached the outside of Alton Park onto Broad Street. There we passed by some policemen on a corner. One cop looked right at us. I could see his face and remember thinking there might be concern. I hope he cared. He knew we were hurt. They saw us, but they just watched us go by. What were they doing just standing there? People were being beaten in there, getting hurt badly. They should have been going in there to help us, shouldn't they?

They didn't appear to move. They weren't going inside that ghetto, if that's what it was. They were outside on Broad Street watching us, waiting, just stationary, as Jim Lewis drove frantically, but carefully, to the Memorial Hospital Emergency Room. I hoped he wouldn't pass out before we got there.

Jim said later he took us to Memorial because he thought Erlanger would be overrun, and he was right. Both hospital emergency rooms were busy all night. Half of us ended up in Erlanger, the other half in Memorial. There, they put me in a small, quiet room and left me alone for what seemed like forever. God, that was horrible! I was crazy with fear. It was at least an hour or more before I finally got up and walked out, so I wouldn't go crazy.

They put me back in there and x-rayed my hand. It was broken, and they put it in a cast. My face was smashed, lip cut and swollen, my teeth loose. But that was all. I was trying to find out about my brother. I was worried and afraid for him. That was the worst thing of all, lying there in that hospital bed not knowing who was killed and who wasn't. Who made it out and who didn't?

Mrs. Ward was in the waiting room. John David Curry, one of the youngest Harlequins, saw her there. She was rubbing her eyes, her head down, shaking and saying, "Why did they do that? Why?" John told me that, recently. We were at a party. It was the first time I'd seen him in forty years. I never saw Mrs. Ward that night after the show started, and I didn't see her at the hospital, either. It must have been awful for her.

I remember seeing people milling around in the corridor. Some wore suits. I don't know who they were, maybe a few reporters. I think Dennis Haskins, who later portrayed Mr. Belding on the TV series *Saved By the Bell*, was talking to them. He must have been all right.

"We aren't supposed to say anything," someone said to me. I wondered why. Then, I thought, why is Dennis talking to reporters? Somebody connected with the University was there somewhere, I guess, and said we weren't supposed to talk to reporters.

Where is Bo Robinson? Is Jim Steele okay? Did they kill Duffy? I should have helped him more. I should have helped Jim Steele. Oh, God, I hope he's not dead! Is Duffy OK? Oh, God! Where's Paul? Please God, please make Paul all right. Please look after him. That's the way it went. That's what it was like for me. That's what I recall happening that night.

The above is my testimony, the story of what happened, at least as far as I remember it. I never had the opportunity to have my say in court, to give my testimony about it there. It's never been written down until now. In court, they asked only vague, broad overview questions like, "Were you beaten?" and "Did more than twenty people attack your group?" They asked those types of questions that required only "yes" and "no" answers. What I've written is what I remember as the truth. A great deal more went on during the melee. But, I don't know about that, so I've only written what I know to be true, what I experienced. I'm telling it for the truth.

Later, my brother related that he was taken, bleeding, with our cousin Barry Walsh and maybe John Gerhing, into several homes in Alton Park. They were rescued by black families and protected, hidden, and then moved again and again, until they were able to get out and to the hospital. Kind black men and women saved them and somehow got them out.

The court cases and trials pertaining to all this began in the fall. By then, Jim Steele's injuries had healed, as had those of all the rest of the Harlequins. Amazingly, there were no other long-term injuries except to my brother Paul. His was the most serious.

Large crowds gathered in bustling waiting rooms. Many people came forward voluntarily and wanted to testify. People were outraged and committed to telling what took place, what they saw, and who was involved. Many kind black citizens were appalled. They wanted to make it right. There were dozens and dozens of witnesses—good people, old people, middle-aged black men and women who came forward to tell the truth about what happened that evening in Alton Park.

The trial went on for days and weeks. Gradually, fewer and fewer people attended court. As time went on, weeks turned into months. It seemed like we had to be there every Tuesday and Thursday, sometimes Wednesdays and Fridays as well. Somehow, we arranged our classes and tests around this major activity in our lives. Every day for three or four months, we got dressed and went to court, though many days it was postponed. It was my senior year in college, and I was trying to prepare for my English comprehensive exams. Going to court nearly every day during the first semester of my senior year was just as crazy as any other part of this story.

However, nothing much really happened. That's the most educational thing about it. That is, until near the end. The Harlequin Massacre was hushed up. It wasn't covered at all by the local media in Chattanooga. Nevertheless, it did make the national CBS Evening News. Probably it was the result of Dennis Haskins answering those questions in the hospital corridor, but I don't really know for sure.

As a member of the group that was attacked, I never really

understood why it occurred, or even exactly what happened. As the seminal event of my college education, it certainly is one of the pivotal events in my life and the lives of fifteen or so other young, white, theater students, the Harlequins.

Perhaps it was as equally disturbing in the lives of the three- or four-hundred black citizens, young and old, who witnessed it—not to mention the forty to fifty or so young black men and women who attacked us, although only two were ever convicted of anything.

I don't think any of those folks will ever forget this event, either. I do know for a fact, that all those white actors who were attacked that day forty years ago in Alton Park Homes in Chattanooga will never forget that summer evening in 1971.

A few days later, perhaps a week after the attack, I was sitting in the stands at Warner Park. Some of my other brothers and sisters were sitting next to my mother and me. We were watching a swimming meet. My face still hurt, and my hand was in a cast. I remember suddenly seeing Jim Steele's face; all of a sudden it just appeared to me. He was getting pummeled, again and again. His head jerking back, his hair whipping around, the blood spurting out of his face and his eyes shut! I looked again, and they were swimming. I've seen that image all my life. I wish I could make it go away.

What happened, how it was handled, and the ramifications have been a mystery not just to my family and me, but to a lot of other people as well. Our interpretation of the events that transpired in Alton Park may be terribly inaccurate. But it's all we have available to try to make sense of it all.

For nearly two-thirds of my life this event has been like an inscrutable puzzle to me. The truth about what happened, the information about it, has been inaccessible. Perhaps that's my own choice. Maybe information about what happened hasn't been unattainable; maybe I just haven't actually tried to find out what happened and why. Maybe a better question is, do I really want to know?

Frankly, the answer is yes. I would like to know what happened. I need to know and think a lot of other people would like to know. We would like to know how this affected all the other participants. I'd like to hear their individual stories, too, from both those attacked and the attackers.

After working a career in television journalism as a TV producer of *The Heartland Series*, I'd like to know and am ready to find out how this event shaped and affected the lives of everyone involved. What was going on in the minds of all the participants that night? Were they in Alton Park to attend a meeting of the Black Panther Party that late afternoon? What triggered this event? Was it planned? Could it have been avoided? What effect, if any, has it had on their subsequent lives and why?

It would also be valuable to understand the thinking of the University's handling of this, as well as the city's motives and maneuverings in dealing with the case. Why was it handled the way that it was?

It would be interesting to understand the pressures that Coach Henry Bowles faced during these events. What was he up against? Why didn't he just come forward from the first and testify? Why did he delay? What did he endure from his community when he finally did come forward and testify? It was at the end of the trial when he corroborated the testimony of two witnesses, identifying the two who were convicted. And what was his thinking the night of the riot; why didn't he allow us to leave when we had the chance? Or was it up to Mrs. Ward to make that decision?

For forty years, these and many other questions have remained unanswered. One such question I have often been asked is, in a riot with such wholesale violence, why were only two people convicted?

It's my hope that this incident can be studied further. I would like to develop a documentary about the history of the Harlequins, including this riot at the Spencer McCallie Homes in Alton Park in 1971. It should include all the participants still living: the audience that night, the attackers, the actors, teachers, and city employees. All could be approached and interviewed, providing a very important television documentary that publically explores unanswered questions.

Epilogue

When I finally got out of the hospital that night in 1971, I went home. The next day I awoke with every bone in my body hurting, aching from the beating the night before. But at least I wasn't still in the hospital.

My brother, Paul, wasn't home when I woke up. Neither was my mother. She was back at the hospital with him. As soon as I could, I went to the Erlanger Hospital. That's where they had taken Paul. When I arrived, I entered a crowded hospital room where my mother was with my brother. It was a ward room. There were ten or fifteen beds full of patients lined up on either side of a long room. Many of the ill were very old, some on ventilators. The room smelled of age, medicines, and urine.

I crossed the foot of many beds, moving down the room and looking at the patients. It wasn't a wide room, just wide enough for patients to be wheeled in and out and to walk. It was like a crowded dorm room, and I could see my mother standing at the far end of the room at a bedside.

There lay my little brother, Paul. He was around fifteen at the time, and his head was wrapped with a huge, clean, white bandage. It came down to his eyebrows, and reached up like a turban. He still had dried blood on his lips. He was asleep, thank God.

My mother told me he'd come home from the hospital. He'd been with Barry, our cousin. Some black families had hidden him and moved him to other homes until they got him to the hospital. At Erlanger he'd been checked and then discharged. However, he kept throwing up during the night, so she brought him back to the hospital. They immediately called in Dr. Walter Boehm, a family friend, who luckily for Paul also happened to be one of the best brain surgeons in Chattanooga at the time. My mother sure thought he was.

Dr. Boehm operated on my brother and removed a piece of his skull. It had broken off when he was hit with a lead pipe. The prognosis was good and, with luck, Paul would recover and heal.

I left Erlanger Hospital and headed down Third Street toward the University. It was only about a mile from there to campus. It was quiet. On the way, I couldn't help but worry. I kept seeing the image of my mother leaning over Paul's bed and wondering, hoping that he would open his eyes again, but not knowing if he would. Damn.

He had been at the Spencer McCallie Homes just to watch a children's play, to see his big brother perform for other children. He'd gotten his head split open with a lead pipe while sitting in a car waiting to leave. Now he could die because of it. Why? Why would anybody want to hurt a child like this?

These were my thoughts as I approached the on-campus home of the University of Chattanooga president. His home was a very nice but modest brick structure with a garden. I remember the big trees in the yard. It was a block from St. Swithen's Hall, where Duffy's apartment was located.

I knocked on the door and, when an older woman answered, I asked to see the president. His wife, I presume. She didn't hesitate going to get her husband and left me standing in the doorway. I don't remember if she asked me in or not; I think she did, but I declined.

When the president came to the door, I told him who I was and where I'd been the night before. He knew about what had happened, but he let me finish. I told him that my brother Paul was lying in a hospital room with twenty other patients and that he might not recover. I didn't want my mother or my brother to be in there with all those other patients.

I asked him if he thought that was right. I told him it would be better if he could see to it that my brother be moved to a smaller room where he could get better care. He said he would. I don't know what I would have done if he had said he couldn't. Then, I left. I went back to the hospital. There wasn't any place else to go.

Charlie Garland's Stove

This story has been told and retold for more than one hundred years, ever since it happened. We first heard it soon after we began doing *The Heartland Series*. However, it took us nearly twenty years to find someone we could talk into carrying a stove around all day before we could film the story. Actually, the real reasons we couldn't do the story were that we couldn't figure out how to shoot it, and we couldn't find a stove light enough for somebody to carry around all day while we took pictures of them.

It wasn't until we met a prop maker at the Clarence Brown Theater, Christy Fogarty, that we were able to tell the story. She made us an exact replica of the actual stove. I still have that stove in my house; its sitting right here by my desk as I type.

The prop stove was made out of a light balsa wood and painted black. It still weighed nearly fifty-five pounds. After Ernie Proffitt carried it around all day while we shot the story, it felt like it weighed 217 pounds, which is the actual weight of the stove Charlie carried.

Charlie Garland was probably the strongest man who ever lived in Cades Cove. He was legendary strong. His feats of strength have survived for one-hundred years in their telling and retelling. Charlie wasn't an exceptionally large man. Having heard about him for so long, we thought he had to be a mountain of a man, but he wasn't. He did have huge thighs and immensely strong legs. He was known for his speed, too. He was just less than six-feet tall, probably about five-feet-eleven-inches tall, and he weighed a little less than two-hundred pounds.

Folks still say that if you needed some help in setting up a cane mill or apple press or anything that required exceptional strength, Charlie was your man. Folks just looked to Charlie for help. With Charlie's help you didn't need support from anyone else.

Charlie lived in the Beard Cane. That's what they called the section of the Smoky Mountains where the Garlands lived. Some called it the Hurricane. It's up one of the hollers from Cades Cove, the beautiful, remote mountain valley.

Today, it's hard hiking to the Beard Cane. You can get there from Cades Cove or drop down from the Top of the World section and hike into it. Also, from Abrams Creek on the south side of the Park, you get there by hiking along Cooper Mountain Road. It's about seven miles from that direction. From Cades Cove, it's a hard six miles into the Beard Cane, maybe more. It's pretty snaky in there, I've heard. I've never been in there myself.

Some of Charlie Garland's feats of strength are remarkable. Once, he carried seven bushels of corn three miles up a mountain. He did this by putting three and half bushels in each of two sheets, then hung the sheets together around his neck. It was like carrying a yoke with two buckets of water on a pole around his neck.

The point is he did it. A bushel of corn weighs about seventy or seventy-two pounds. Throw in the fact that he climbed three miles up a mountain with it, and it's a feat that is un-duplicable—if there is such a word. It'll never be repeated. Nobody can carry five-hundred pounds around his neck while climbing three miles up a mountain. But Charlie could, and Charlie did. Whew!

Charlie is reputed to have at least two big, wild sons named Jake and Jim. A picture exists of them and some others standing in front of the Blount County jail in Maryville. There are others in the picture, too, standing by an old still.

Jake was a bigger man than his daddy, taller in size from what I've heard. After a drinking spell once, Jake came home a-figurin' on taking on the old man, wrastlin' to see who was the better man, so the story goes according to Virgil Garland. After repeatedly telling his son to stop messing with him, Charlie finally grabbed Jake by the belt and the scruff of the neck, picked him up, and scrubbed the ceiling with him, supposedly like you would use a rag, back and forth, belly–side up, across the ceiling before he dropped him. Jake never messed with Charlie again after that. These were tough, strong people.

Another story about Jake involves the Blount County jail and the notorious so-called "Kangaroo Court." The law needed

Bill Dunlap, prisoners Jake and Jim Garland and three others by Maryville jail, 1914

somebody to go undercover inside the jail to "clean up the rackets" that were being run by a dangerous tough bunch who were intimidating everybody locked up inside the jail. Jake and his brother Jim were known to have dabbled in the liquor trade, so the Blount County sheriff locked Jake up to straighten out the mess inside the jail without the sheriff having to do anything about it. Jake was ready when the leader of the "bad bunch" came after him, for he had taken off his hob-nailed boot. When the leader of this oppressive gang came for him, Jake let him have it across the face with the heel of his boot. And with teeth a-flying, that's all it took. With the situation now under control, the sheriff was pleased to promptly remove Jake from his incarceration.

We were fortunate to meet and talk with many of the Garland family, including Virgil Garland, who lived near Lanier, which is near Pumpkin Center out Highway 129 toward Chilhowie Dam. Virgil was Charlie's grandson or great nephew, and he was in his 80s when we got to talk to him.

Another member of the Garland family, Jake's son-in-law,

told us another story. He visited Jake in the hospital near the end of his life. It was one of the only times Jake was ever in a hospital. Jake was getting old and very sick. During his visit, Jake's son-in-law got old Jake up out of bed to walk him to the bathroom. Of course, with the good plumbing in the hospital, the toilet had water in it. As Jake shuffled over and saw the toilet, he stopped in the doorway and said, "Damn it, I told those people to empty that thing!"

But it's Jake's father, Charlie, who carried the stove that I started to tell about, and I'm telling this for the truth. The stove in question is one of those old kitchen stoves, a step-stove, they're called. They were commonly used in the early 20th century to heat the kitchen in the morning. This story occurred around 1903. The Garland family showed me an authentic 1903 Sears-Roebuck catalogue with pictures of similar stoves, if not the exact one that Charlie carried. It is listed as a cast-iron kitchen step-stove. It cost around four dollars and thirty-seven cents then. The stove weighed 217 pounds.

Charlie Garland had gone to town that day to the Cauldell (or Caldwell) Hardware store in downtown Maryville for the sole purpose of buying a stove. Charlie had walked, as he usually did everywhere he went. He had come to town from the Beard Cane, a distance of about seventeen miles. This particular day, Charlie brought with him two tote sacks and a "hank" of rope. The man at the hardware store saw Charlie, and probably knew him, and when he asked Charlie what he wanted, Charlie said, "I need that stove right there."

"Fine," the man said, "Just pull your wagon around back, and we'll load it up for you."

"I didn't bring a wagon with me."

"Well, how'd you get to town, then?" the man asked.

"Walked," Charlie answered.

"And, how do you plan on getting that thing, the stove, home?"

"I'm going to carry it," is what Charlie replied.

"You're not going to carry THAT stove, not that stove, Charlie. Not back to the Beard Cane, you aren't, Charlie. That stove weighs 217 pounds!"

The hardware man, the owner of the store, and Charlie must have discussed this for some time. Charlie showed them the rope

Charlie's stove

he'd brought and two burlap sacks. He'd brought them in order to strap the stove across his back and tie it so the stove wouldn't rub the hide off his big back.

"I'll tell you what. I'll tell you what I'm going to do," the hardware man said. "If you carry that stove all the way home without ever putting it down, I'll just give it to you."

"Fine," said Charlie. "Will you throw in those pots and pans?"

"Yeah, I'll through in that skillet, too! You can tie 'em up inside the stove. But you can't put it down. Not once. If you do, you have to pay for it."

Charlie agreed. They had a bargain. The hardware man put the pots, pans, and skillet inside the stove. I suppose they rattled around some, but Charlie carried them.

And that's the way it went that day in 1903, or pretty near it. The owner of the hardware store sent another employee along on horseback. He was to follow Charlie that day to make sure the bargain was kept.

When the *Heartland* crew shot this story, we didn't have a horse. But, we had the next best thing: Dale Kelly. I say this with all due respect! The reason is that Dale Kelly is probably the strongest man in Happy Valley, maybe even the whole of Blount

County, where most of this *Heartland* story was shot. Dale's even stronger than Ernie Proffitt, who carried the stove for us when we shot the story. But, Dale isn't quite the actor Ernie is! Anyway, that's how it was done, how we shot this story. Ernie Proffitt portrayed Charlie Garland, who carried the stove strapped to his back. Dale Kelly followed Ernie around all that day.

Our job was to research and figure out historically the route that Charlie would actually have taken. We would shoot the terrain, the mountains, and the creek-crossings and show how difficult the feat really was. The Garland family helped us with this, along with Gordon E. Wright, Sr. and Judy Hill, who knew the story and the country Charlie traveled through to get back home. He must have traveled out of Maryville from the hardware store on Wilkerson Pike, which maybe didn't exist then. The route he probably took was out Tuckaleechee Pike on the old Whites Mill Road to Walland Gap.

Crossing creeks, he would come to Piney Flatts, or Piney Level, as it's called. From there, he would begin to climb and cross over many mountains to get over and through the Chilhowie mountain chain. The easiest, most level route from Walland Gap was probably up through Miller's Cove, where he would reach Blair Branch near Blackberry Farms. From there he would cross over Blair Gap and drop down into the Hurricane, as it was often called then. Today, it's called the Beard Cane, where Charlie lived.

All the time he traveled, the hardware man followed him on horseback. This is a fact. Charlie did lean against a tree once or twice, but he never once put that stove down. We figured he needed water. So, when we shot the story, we had Dale give Ernie a drink or two while leaning the stove against a tree. The leaning part is historically accurate. Charlie Garland was the strongest man who ever lived in the Cove. And they still tell this tale about him.

Ernie Proffitt, the man who portrayed Charlie, is a contractor, a block and stone mason, and a friend who helped me build my cabin in Happy Valley at Abrams Creek. Ernie looks amazingly just like Charlie Garland. So, it was a good choice. We found a single picture of Charlie, who could be Ernie's uncle or pap. They look that much alike.

From the Top of the World, up near Look Rock, are beautiful views of the Smoky Mountains. From there, you can see the rugged mountains that Charlie carried that stove up and over, and up and over again. It's unbelievable. You have to see the country to appreciate Charlie's accomplishment. That's why we went up there. That's where he traveled. That's what we tried to do in telling the story for *The Heartland Series.* We wanted to show the audience what Charlie did and where he did it, and what he had to do to get that stove home. It's a story that will live on and be retold again and again for another one-hundred years.

Bill's Little Stories

The first time a businessman from Ohio was in East Tennessee, he got lost. It was up near the Morgan County, Wartburg area. There used to be an old country store there. When the businessman went into the store to get directions, there was a barefoot country boy by the door eating goober peanuts out of a gallon jug. He was eating one right after another.

Well, the businessman got his directions and started back out the door when he noticed the country boy and said, real fast, like those Northerners talk, "Hey, son, do you think it's a good idea you eating peanuts like that, one right after another?"

The little boy just kept eating them, looked up from the jug, and said, "My granddaddy lived to be ninety-four years old."

"Did he eat a lot of peanuts?" the businessman asked.

"No," the little country boy said. "He minded his own business!"

Howard Baker Stories

One afternoon we went to visit Howard Baker at his home in Huntsville, Tennessee. Overlooking a gorge above the Big South Fork River, we talked to him on his porch one spring day.

Scott County is where Howard Baker grew up, and that's where his heart is. We asked him "How come after all you've done—after you served President Reagan as his Chief of Staff, distinguished yourself on the Watergate Commission, served as Senate minority leader, and traveled the world—you always come back to little old Huntsville, Tennessee?"

"Because," he said smiling, "Huntsville is the center of the universe. That's where my taproot is!"

Here are a few wonderful tales he told us that afternoon.

He said he was twelve years old before he found out everyone's grandmother didn't hide a pearl-handled revolver under her pillow.

Howard once took his grandson with him to an event at the White House. The press was there, photographers and cameras everywhere. It was a big event that feted Senator Baker, celebrating his career near the end of his public life. He said it was a big fuss about him. On the way home, in the quiet of his car, Howard's grandson looked at him and asked, "Popee, did you used to be somebody?"

On the wall of Howard Baker's home is a wonderful childhood picture of him and his two best friends when he was growing up. The three of them remained steadfast friends all their lives. The picture looks like that old photo of country boys talking about how the crops are doing, taken from the back. Only this photo is face front.

Howard said he and his friends even tried going into business together, but it didn't work out. They partnered up while Howard was in college. "It was a farm scheme," he called it. His buddy called him up and said they had the prettiest broccoli patch in the whole county and all he needed for a bumper crop was one big load of fertilizer, how 'bout it? Well, Howard couldn't say no to his best buddy. Besides, it was a farm project that would help the county. So, Howard sent the money for the fertilizer.

The next time he got home, they went out to the field together to check the crop. Howard found the ground hardened like brick and white as snow. There were no plants coming up anywhere. Howard said his partner had fertilized his broccoli with cement! He had the only concrete broccoli crop ever grown in Scott County. That was the last farm venture he tried with his longtime friend. They stayed friends as long as they didn't partner up in farm schemes.

One last story involves Senator Everett Dirkson, Howard's father-in-law. It was a little exchange Howard had with him one night driving home together from the White House. Howard has used this anecdote in many a speech and impromptu talk.

It was another event that featured an award for Howard, the National Heritage Medal or something. It was a typical Washington highbrow event with photographers, tuxedos, etc. Senator Dirkson was driving. He looked over at Howard and could see that "I was certainly full of myself."

"You know, Howard, the number of people that attend your funeral," he said very slowly, "depends largely on the weather!"

Howard Baker rose to the top of his profession from his roots in Scott County. He continues living today in Huntsville, Tennessee, where his taproot is.

The Great River Adventure

There are two kinds of time in the river. High water when it rains, and low water when it don't.
  —Tommy Utter, riverboat captain

He turned the sea into dry land, they passed through the waters on foot—come, let us rejoice in him. . . . Praise our God, he has preserved our lives and kept our feet from slipping. For you, O God, tested us; you refined us like silver. You brought us into prison and laid burdens on our backs. You let men ride over our heads; we went through fire and water, but you brought us to a place of abundance. I will come to your temple with burnt offerings and fulfill my vows to you—vows my lips promised and my mouth spoke when I was in trouble.
  —Psalm 66 (NIV)

It's early April and the fish are biting! So I'm thinking to myself, "It's been another hard week of work on *The Heartland Series.* I've been doing this, and I've been doing that. I'm beat! I've been working fourteen-hour days all spring. I'm tired. I'm going fishing. I've earned it, deserve it, and I'm going!"

Thinking back on it now, twenty years later, it's just this kind of attitude that gets me into trouble—the "I want it, and I want it now" kind of attitude where I can't be reasoned with. It always leads to bad things. I don't know about you, but when I get tired, I get selfish as well. Not just self-centered and stubborn, but stupid, too. When I get this way, I can make bad decisions, the kind that lead to real trouble. But never before has it led to anything like the story I'm about to tell.

This is the story of a great river adventure during which I almost lost my life and the lives of my sixteen-year-old son, Jack, his best friend, Gabe Gagliardi, and my fishing buddy, Sammy

Tillery, on what was supposed to be a simple little canoe trip down Abrams Creek in the Great Smoky Mountains (see Plates 31 and 32).

Sammy Tillery is a great friend of mine who used to live across the street in the Rocky Hill neighborhood in Knoxville. He and I have fished all over East Tennessee on all types of rivers: the Clinch, the Obed, even the Big South Fork, where we nearly drowned once in high water. On that trip we lost everything including our canoes. But this trip would be different. We didn't want any trouble. We weren't planning on doing anything remotely dangerous, like whitewater rafting. We were just out for a nice easy float to fish with my son and his friend, something like a three-hour tour.

We were set to go on Saturday. It's a seven-mile trip along Abrams Creek from the Abrams Creek ranger station to Chilhowee Lake. Sammy had a canoe, and I rented one from Riversports. We slapped them onto our vehicles, and off we went. No, sir—no work, no camera crew today. We're going fishing, yee-ha!

Abrams Creek, on the backside of the Great Smoky Mountains National Park, flows out of Cades Cove. It's spectacularly beautiful in April, as cool and shiny clear as October's bright blue weather (see Plate 19).

The waters are high in April. In fact, the spring rains had caused dangerous flooding a few weeks before our trip. All the streams flowing through Cades Cove – tributaries like Mill Creek, Anthony Creek, and Rounds Creek – were all full, the runoff glistening in the bright spring sun.

These streams gather in Cades Cove to form the headwaters of Abrams Creek. At the east end of the Cove, near Becky Cable Mill, they all join together. From Cades Cove, Abrams flows about three miles through the mountains to Abrams Falls. Then, it flows another five miles down the mountains to Abrams Creek Campground where we planned to put in. It's right near the Happy Valley community, which is only a ridge or two over from the creek. From Abrams Creek Campground the creek flows another seven miles until it empties into Chilhowee Lake. It's the seven-mile stretch from the campground to the embayment that we wanted to fish. At least that's what we thought we were going to do.

There are only two places to put a canoe into Abrams Creek: in the Park at the campground or at the mouth of the creek, about a mile-and-a-half down at Chilhowee Lake Bridge on 129. The put-in place is just inside the National Park near the community of Happy Valley. You can get there two ways, either by going over Chilhowee Mountain by way of Montvale Road, or by traveling 411 from Maryville, Tennessee, then State Highway 129, the road to Fontana Resort. This road is also called The Tail of the Dragon, a famous windy road where motorcyclists frequently have accidents due to its 318 curves in the space of eleven miles. I hate to drive that road both ways on the same day. If I have to, it always makes me sick.

I hadn't felt good about the weather on Friday. How could I? It had already rained two inches and was still raining as I was sitting in my car. I asked the young, athletic fellow, who was tying my canoe onto my car, what the river looked like. "It looks beautiful," he said cheerily. "We canoed it just last week before all this rain. By Monday it will be perfect again." I thought to myself, "By Monday, he said, but we're going Saturday."

We arrived at the river at nine a.m. Saturday, April 12th. The boys slept late; I couldn't get them up. They each had a piece of toast for breakfast. Gabe rode with me, and Jack with Sammy. Both boys were about sixteen and wanted to drive everywhere, but since we were crossing semi-dangerous Chilhowee Mountain and were in a hurry, we told them they could drive home later.

During the ride down, I told Gabe that every time old Sammy and I got together we had an adventure! Sammy told me later that he told Jack the same thing. We stopped on the way and picked up some bread, sandwich meat, chips, and cokes and put them in Sammy's trusty little cooler, which has been a long way with us on all our adventures. We always take it along. The boys thought we were very smart to think ahead.

It was a cool April morning, all right, as we unloaded canoes at the campground along with our fishing gear, poles, lunch, drinks, ice, even a camera, which we put in Sammy's waterproofed wet bag. We left the boys working on our fishing gear, getting everything packed and ready. We took both vehicles—my little four-wheel drive Suzuki and Sammy's truck. Then, we drove about five miles to the other end of Happy Valley to Chilhowee Lake.

My Suzuki would be our pick-up car. We were going to leave it at the bridge on 129 where we would arrive later. But, as we drove by, we decided to go ahead and drive two more miles to Tallassee General Store, as Sammy wanted some film for his camera.

This also gave us the opportunity to drive by and see the final section of our float from the road where the creek flows into Abrams Creek embankment. It would be the last quiet mile-and-a-half of our trip. It's where the rapids end and the calm water starts and continues all the way to where Abrams Creek meets Chilhowee Lake. This last mile-and-a-half would be the slowest, most time-consuming part of our adventure, we thought. We'd probably get tired of paddling here. But something else caught our attention. There seemed to be a whole lot of water in the creek, and the lake was way up, too.

We walked into the old country store at Tallassee right below Chilhowee Dam. It's a great store, serving folks from Pumpkin Center to the Dragon; it's also the local post office for the community. Upon entering, we told the guys hanging around that we were thinking about doing some fishing.

I knew the guy at the cash register, Charlie. There were five or six other locals standing around, too. One guy was chewing tobacco, one had a cigarette, and there was an old grizzled-looking fellow who had his arms folded, and who for some reason kept looking at me, staring me right in the eye.

He said, "It will take five or six hours to float it" — not the four hours we'd been told. He looked like he had plenty of good, common sense. But there was something else about his demeanor. It might have been his wisdom or confidence. He seemed to know something we didn't, like he had an intuitive knowledge or a foreshadowing. Actually, he looked gravely concerned. He looked straight at me as Charlie, who was still behind the cash register, asked, "Where you going to fish?"

"Abrams Creek," I said, "We're going to float it."

"You gonna float it, huh? Little high?" Charlie sort of cocked his head to one side, as he rang something up. Everybody standing around could hear what was being said. They were all no doubt in on the entire conversation, and we wanted them to be. We were trying to find out all we could about this place and where we were going on our trip. So I turned to them and started talking.

"Yeah," I said, "We're going to do some smallmouth fishing down Abrams Creek. We're going to float it, and . . ." Before I could finish, the old grizzled-whiskered guy cut me off.

"There's a lot of water in thar." He had a gravelly, scratchy voice. He sounded kind of tired. He said it again, "Aaghh, there's a lot a water in thar."

Somewhat startled, I said, "You think it's, uh, too high to try to float it?"

He just cocked his head as if to say maybe or he didn't know. I couldn't tell which. I started talking again, and said, "We're going to take our boys in there . . ." Again, slowly, in that gravelly voice, he cut me off.

"You gonna take boys in thar?" I started to respond, but before I could answer he repeated it again, this time not asking a question. "You gonna take boys in thar! There's a lot of water in thar."

I think he was trying to tell me something, but I wasn't listening. He warned me three times, like the cock crowing, but I didn't heed it, although I thought about it driving back along the Little T to join the boys. We were on our great adventure, and nothing was going to stop us. It was what we wanted to do. We were going to fish. We weren't out to whitewater.

Heading back up 129, passing Chilhowee dam, we could see water cascading over it with great fury, foam, and turbulence. Whoosh! At the foot of the dam, it churned and roared and rushed downstream for its first dangerous one-hundred yards. There was so much water the spillway gates were open. This was another warning.

A hundred times since, I've regretted NOT putting in right there. We could have changed our plans and just fished downstream below the dam. It was simple and accessible. It would have been easy to move our cars. We could catch some nice, clean rainbow trout; it would have been a safe, peaceful float down river. The change in plans would only have cost us about an hour. It would have been simple to repack our gear, re-tie our canoes, and move.

"Sammy, we're going to get wet if we get in Abrams Creek, you know?" He knew. We both knew. "We'll just tie down our gear, and we'll be all right."

That Was Our First Mistake

Back at the campground, the boys were excited and raring to go. They'd put all the weighted hooks in the grubs for bait and packed everything into the canoes. We locked Sammy's truck, hoisted the canoes up onto our shoulders, and started carrying them towards the creek thirty yards away. But, looking up, we saw we weren't alone. We'd attracted a covey of four Boy Scouts. They and their two adult leaders had just arrived and parked next to our truck.

"Where are you headed? Canoeing, huh?" they said with big toothy grins as they ventured by us. "Have you checked the river flow?" the older fellow asked. "Do you know the country you'll be canoeing through?"

Our response to these guys' well-intentioned interrogation was almost friendly — actually, a little condescending. It was more like, "Yeah, yeah, we know all about it." We didn't want to hear it. They were asking questions about our familiarity with the stream and whether we'd checked in with the park ranger.

"Hey," we felt like saying, "this is our trip, and we're going right now. We've fiddle-farted around here long enough." We were about to slide our canoes into the water as the Boy Scouts watched us from the bank.

"Here," Sammy said as he dug his hand into his loosely tied wet-bag and pulled out a camera. He handed it to one of the Boy Scouts, asking, "Could you take a picture of this expedition?" The kid obliged, and we posed for the only picture ever taken of those involved in the Great River Adventure.

"The famous last picture," Sammy said, laughing, and we all laughed, too. Even the Boy Scouts laughed. We didn't know how right Sammy was.

The river was beautiful, but it was full, and fast — too fast. Gabe weighed about one-hundred-eighty pounds, and he was riding in the front of Sammy's canoe. He outweighed Sammy by about fifty pounds. The river was up, way up, and about two-hundred yards downstream Sammy's boat tipped over. Sammy and Gabe lost a paddle, right there.

They were in front of us. Jack and I were also flying downriver. They turned over in a simple rapid in a straight section. We were in it, now. Flying downriver, no paddling – just steering. We finally got to the edge of the channel, turned and angled out of it into a rhododendron thicket, and crashed against the bank with a boom. We jammed the canoe through the river cane into the rock bank with a hard thud. The canoe managed to hold steady. It almost capsized but remained upright without swamping in the fierce current.

Sammy and Gabe were busy bailing water out of their boat and struggling to right their canoe. Looking around, we thought, "What the hell! There aren't any banks at all in this creek." There was no place where you could pull over and stop. We were up to our armpits in water trying to stay on our feet. We started bailing water out of our boat, immediately.

We'd taken on a lot of water through that first fast stretch and had to empty our canoes now or capsize, too. The water was extremely cold. Gabe was wearing shorts. With his teeth chattering, he said, "I think I'd better sit closer to the middle when we start back up." We agreed that was a good idea.

Jack, Sammy, and I were wearing jeans, which were already wet and heavy. While we were stopped, we re-strapped the fishing gear down. This wasn't going to be a gentle float. So, we started to retie everything in earnest, using the duct tape we'd brought, and did a much better job this time. We taped our fishing poles to the gunnels and the thwarts, which are the support sticks that run perpendicularly across the canoe. If the canoes went down, our gear was going to sink with them. This was going to be a little tougher trip than we figured, maybe a lot tougher.

I turned to Sammy, a little worried, "What do you think?"

He said, "We probably ought to get out of here. There's just too much water." We talked about rough-necking the canoes back along what little bank existed upstream. We'd only traveled about two-hundred yards. It was going to be rough sloshing upstream trying to get back to where we started: nothing but overgrowth and bank cover (see Plate 21). Then, we could scrap this trip on the creek, get out, drive down to the lake, and fish there. Or, we could float below the dam for trout.

The boys, meanwhile, were yelling and laughing, jumping up and down and busting each other with chest-bumps. "Wahoo," they yelled, trading high fives and slapping each other! BIG TRIP: whitewater. They loved it! This was our last chance to turn back.

That Was Our Second Mistake

Instead, we decided to continue downstream and pick up Gabe's paddle. It was red so it shouldn't be hard to see. Well, we never saw that paddle again, and we quickly went through three swirling rapids back to back that didn't have any breaks between them. That was what the entire river was like—one long, dangerous, mean rapid!

We were running rapids without flotation devices, one right after the other. I thought we were navigating like pros, doing well, at first. There were no logs in the middle of the creek. It was clear and clean, but flowing fast. The recent big flood had swept through and cleaned out everything.

The first time Jack and I tipped over wasn't fifteen minutes into our journey. Compared to what was coming, it wasn't a particularly harsh section of the river, either. Jack was paddling for all he was worth! I was paddling hard, too; the adrenaline was pumping. But for some reason, the boat veered up and over to the left and instantly filled with water. The next thing we knew, we were in the drink trying to hold on to the canoe, which was careening downstream, upside down with us hanging on top of it!

I couldn't see a thing. It was like I was wearing a loose-fitting diving mask, but it was my clipped-on blueblocker sunglasses. It was like I was going through a carwash! Luckily, they were still hanging onto my head, thanks to a little rope I'd tied around them, but they were full of water. For a while, they remained tied to my head, but not for long. I lost my best sunglasses. Damn, I had those sunglasses for nearly a year, and I can't keep anything for a year. But losing my blueblockers was nothing compared to the seriousness of losing my Batman baseball cap. That's serious. My hat and I had been together for eight or ten years. I always wore it fishing. I can't begin to explain it. Canoeing and fishing were the prime times, the only occasions when I wore my Batman hat. Now, it too was gone!

After turning over our canoes to get the water out, we struggled to get back in them and on our way. Sammy and Gabe did the same. Whew! Early April in the Great Smoky Mountains does NOT mean warm water: the snow in the high elevations was melting and the nights could still get below freezing. Now, paddling downstream into the wind as it whipped through the gorge into our faces, even in the sun, Jack and I were cold in our soggy clothes.

Next thing I knew I was in the same fix as my hat. We were only fifteen or twenty feet from where we'd just been bashed and sloshed when several good-sized breakers and swells broadsided us. Wham, bam! We turned over again. Damn, this was getting frustrating.

We were in the drink again, sailing downstream now. Jack was in front of me. We were both swimming for safety. I was beginning to get scared. The swirling curls, one right after another, were lined up in front of us. We hit them smoothly and squarely, too. It was like sailing along in rough cake batter: those butter-knives, cake-batter curls whipped up atop a cake. But these were alive, churning. It was like navigating along a moving ridgeline: Whoosh! Whoosh!! It was a constant roaring of water. We couldn't pull out, either. We couldn't cut off to one side or the other and head to less violent, less turbulent water. The angle was too great. If we tried, we'd capsize for sure. No, this was the best we could do, frightening as it was because it wasn't good enough. We didn't have a chance!

We had just gotten started, and already we were exhausted. Another concern was that Sammy's boat now had only one paddle. The second time we tipped over we separated and traveled that way until we came upon Gabe, paddling with a big crooked stick! Things were getting primordial.

Of the first three miles we covered, we probably swam nearly a mile of it, which we covered in about an hour. We were like a pair of rockets being shot downriver or getting flushed down a giant toilet bowl. We tipped over four or five times while traveling through the big rapids. When we weren't tipping over, we were submerged in the water, straining to upright the canoes, crashing into the banks, wrestling with canoes, and trying to dump water out. We stopped and dumped water out of our canoes six or seven times. It would have been more, if we had been able to find a place safe that was stable enough to try to right our canoes. These places were few and far between.

The creek was so high it had no banks. There was no easy access to land anywhere; the river's edges were lined with trees, rhododendron, thick reeds, willow thickets, and river cane. When we would finally bang through one of these, we'd crash into a rock wall, which was the mountain side of the gorge. None of these trees, willows, and cane areas looked very deep, but invariably they were. When we tried to dump water out of our canoes, we fell into water up to our armpits. It was always too deep to stand outside of our canoes, even resting against a bank. It shouldn't have been. But it was.

It seemed we were always struggling to keep our footing in waist-deep water. The river always pressured us with its driving, endless, relentless power against whatever we tried to do. The river had a mad life of its own, carrying on its endless flow – completely oblivious to any of our actions. We were like water bugs being washed down a drain. We just didn't matter. Whatever we tried, we were simply up against too great a force. We were insignificant: living human beings, boys, men, and friends. It was as if the gods were laughing at us, "Hey, so what! Take this!! Wham!! This is not your world here. You have no power, authority. You don't have a chance!" That's what nature was saying to us this day on Abrams Creek.

We would separate from the canoes periodically, sometimes for a quarter of a mile or more – swimming, freezing, and getting banged up, hitting the bottom rocks, getting hung up in tree limbs. Once, Jack smashed into a boulder butt first. His feet were up, but the force of the water was too great; he was traveling too fast. Wham! He hit it hard. Finally, about midway, we hit a bank, just washed up. This moment was one of the few times that Sammy, Gabe, Jack, and I were all together on that river.

Our realities were changing. Our perceptions were narrowing. We were completely focused on the single thing that mattered—the rapid in front of us, and how to survive it. How we should position our canoe coming into it. What to do coming out, if we were still upright. There certainly was no time, chance, or possibility of staying in touch with Gabe and Sammy.

It's not that we didn't want to stay near them; we tried. They tried to stay near us, too. We couldn't. We didn't have control of where we were going. We didn't have the luxury of choosing where to dump the water out of our boats when the canoes got full and we were forced to stop and empty them. When we tipped over, we had to start swimming. When our canoes got away from us, which happened often, we had to swim to catch them. We were in a frightening situation.

As best we could figure, we were about four miles from the put-in place at the campground where we started. We had three or four more miles of rapids to go before we reached calm water. When we washed up on the right-hand side of the river this time, Gabe and Sammy were there.

They were alive and relatively unhurt, too. It was certainly good to see them, but I didn't dare tell them that or express it. It would mean the situation was too serious, that we were in real danger, which of course, we were. And it would mean we were scared we might not make it through this hair-brained adventure. At this point in our Great River Adventure, we were just about to give up. We had experienced all the fun we could stand and wanted out. I did. This was just too dangerous.

We still had gear and canoes and, although we were freezing, our adrenaline was still pumping. Our thinking went like this: "We'd better cut our losses and get out of here! We are on the right side of the river. And leave our canoes here? No, we can't leave our canoes, can we?" No. How would we get our canoes out, anyway—$1400 worth of canoes, plus our fishing gear? "Let's try to get through it," we thought. Perhaps we were in shock. Maybe hypothermia had set in, and we weren't thinking correctly, if we ever did.

That Was Our Third Mistake

Here the logistics, the geography of Abrams Creek river flow is important. There is a road that runs from Chilhowee Lake to Happy Valley connecting Abrams Creek Campground to the lake. It runs right through the center of Happy Valley. This road could lead us to safety and out of the hellhole this was starting to become – except hell has no water.

So, for us, the Happy Valley road, in reality, was only two or three ridges over from where we were on the creek. We only had a mile-and-a-half of ridges and wild country to get through to get to the road. The Happy Valley road was starting to sound more to us like a viable option, which is a fancy term for an escape route. However, the far side of the river – the left-hand side of the creek, or whatever you want to call that monster, was a different animal. The left side is much more dangerous and threatening. It's the north side of the river and is remote country.

Over there, on the left-hand side, is the remote Great Smoky Mountains National Park. Its nearby feeder streams, which we would pass traveling downstream, have names like Shotley Branch, Rabbit Creek, and Panther Branch. These are some of the most isolated sections of this wilderness, near the trailhead for Gregory's Bald. On this side of the river, the forest is thick, nearly twenty miles as the crow flies to Fontana Village. But we aren't crows.

Downstream, if we could only get there, is State Highway 129. It's only about four miles. It's remote, uninhabited Smoky Mountains backcountry which wild boar and black bear inhabit (see Plates 27 and 28). These are the wild mountains that Wiley Oakley and the old mountaineers told tales about. Here are rhododendron plants forty-feet tall, dog hobbles, tangled up in the steep gorge lands surrounding Abrams Creek. It's a waterway that has taken eons to form, viciously carving its route over millions of years. There aren't even hunting trails through here. Hunting is not allowed, of course. This is the back side of the National Park. Hikers have more sense than to go into this wild, remote country with no trails, no logging roads, and no accessibility.

Sadly, that's where we ended up. But, I'm getting ahead of myself. We continued canoeing down the river as best we could, if that's what you want to call it. Tumbling down the river might be a better description. We'd been at it now for about three hours—doing nothing but fighting whitewater to stay alive. We were cold, tired, and sore from banging into rocks while swimming out of control downriver. We were also sore and exhausted from trying to break our canoes free from the powerful hydraulics, which can hold an overturned canoe in their vice-grip forever.

The power of rushing water is incredible. Often our canoe got stuck, pinned against a rock on one side with powerful, rushing water on the other. Sometimes it was against a tree or log. When this happened, we'd try to get air under the boats so they would "pop" up and slide free. But we couldn't get any air under the canoes; it just wasn't happening.

For the umpteenth time, Jack and I tipped over and were roaring through whitewater. Jack was screaming, "Let go of the canoe!" I was riding it, flying downstream like riding a bronco instead of the upturned canoe. If it weren't so dangerous, it would have been fun, even funny. Finally, after going through another class three or four rapid, the canoe smashed against a tree with a "Bang!" Jack was screaming, "Let go of the canoe!! Dad, let go!!"

My hand was numb, frozen I guess. As the upturned canoe was slogging around, I somehow ended up in front of it. Whether this happened five minutes or fifty minutes after the last time the canoe tipped, I don't have a clue. Time is always NOW in situations like this, and we had been in this situation for over three hours. I was trying to grab hold of something, anything, as I was floating, going very fast downriver. With Jack still screaming for me to let go of the canoe, I managed to grab hold of a rock, a boulder, or something as I was flying by. But when I did, because of the speed it was traveling, and with the weight of the water inside it, the canoe slammed into my hand, pinning it against a boulder. "Oh man!" It had the weight and force of two tons or more of water behind it. It hurt, but not as much as it should have; because the water was so cold I couldn't feel it entirely. I could see a small cut at the base of my ring finger, and my wedding ring now looked like it was sitting between two big doughnuts.

I held on and managed to get the head rope around a tree, six or eight feet upstream from where the canoe was lodged.

The water was three-feet deep, but the force of the current made standing impossible. With all my strength against the force of the water, I managed to tie off the rope onto an upstream tree. At least now the canoe couldn't get loose and be pulled down river, but the canoe was starting to bend a bit.

Jack finally got to me by land, crashing through the laurel and rhododendron. He now had a serious look on his face. He was all business. At the edge of the stream, he slid down the bank and entered the water above me. I was still straining to keep hold of the canoe-rope tied around an upriver tree. I was about to give up and let go. I just couldn't hold it anymore. But with Jack's help pulling on the rope, we managed after ten minutes of straining to turn the canoe over. It had about half the river running through it. But when it caught some air, it finally popped up, even though it still had four or five inches of water in it. At least now we could lift it over our heads and empty it.

All the time we were working on the canoe, we were running in place underwater. Our feet could barely be called secure. We weren't standing in water—more like sitting in it, lolling, rolling around trying to get some leverage.

We got back into our canoe—there wasn't anything else we could do—and continued downriver. Immediately, we fell into a real bad section. As Jack and I righted ourselves and looked downriver, we could see Sammy at the foot of a giant wall of timber. His canoe had somehow lodged into the base of a forty to fifty-foot-wide pile of huge timbers. It was like a log dam. The wood was about ten to fifteen-feet high, sticking out like so many pick-up sticks above the water.

Here, the river or creek, whatever you want to call it, takes a sharp left turn. Because of the awesome flooding, debris from all sorts of tree limbs, including whole trees, had washed free. Everything in the forest coming down the river was getting caught here. It was being swept downriver into what looked like a giant beaver dam.

As Jack and I paddled up to this spot on the river, we saw Sammy standing high atop this enormous pile of logs, perched above his red canoe, pulling, yanking on a rope trying to shake the canoe free. With the water's tremendous hydraulic power, the canoe had been driven deep into this log mountain. Sammy wasn't having much luck getting it out, but as luck would have it, we crashed into a tree-lined bank just upstream from Sammy.

We tied off at the base of the logjam and climbed across the tumble of logs to reach him. We didn't see Gabe anywhere. Jack and I scampered across the slick logs like a couple of squirrels, and after a few near disasters, we reached Sammy. When he looked up, he smiled, and immediately we could see blood all over his face. We were horrified. The blood was coming from a cut above his eye. He could barely stand up; he was shaking convulsively in large epileptic-like movements. He didn't look good at all.

Sammy is slightly built without much meat on him. He was shaking so badly he wasn't able to work his canoe free. The thwarts, the pieces of wood that stabilize a canoe, were broken. The wet bag was soaked and too heavy to pull out of the canoe. Both the front and rear ropes were tied to broken thwarts. Sammy's fishing gear looked to be in pretty bad shape, too. One pole was broken, and pieces were still among the ropes. But it didn't matter, because we weren't going to be doing much fishing on this trip anytime soon.

Sammy's canoe had a big dent in it. We thought we might get it out if we could get the canoe free from the trees. We yanked and tried and tried, but it wouldn't budge. How could it? Half the river was pinning it against the logjam. We crawled around on the logjam for nearly an hour. We struggled and strained and finally looked for a log to use as a lever. With timber stacked thirty-feet high, we didn't have much trouble locating something we could use to dislodge the canoe. Grabbing a long, straight maple pole, we fed it through the debris. Now we had a tool. We positioned it against another larger log just above the little red canoe. The make-shift lever was twenty-five-feet long and nearly six-inches thick.

While Sammy pulled on a rope from one end, I pulled from the other end, and Jack worked the lever in between. We finally managed to move the canoe enough to get a little air under it. When it moved even a little bit, it stirred a ray of hope in us. Exhausted, there were times we wanted to give up, but renewed by the possibility of succeeding with this half-baked maneuver, we felt we could do it. WE HAD TO DO IT to get that damned canoe free!

Each little movement was a small victory. We would gain a few inches and tie it off. We'd loosen the rope, pull, and re-tie the ropes. This was the only way to offset the continuous river pressure, and pulling and pushing like a trio of stevedores, we finally shook that canoe free, and it rolled over. When this happened, the air popped inside it, and it pulled loose and was free! It was as if we'd accomplished the impossible, and we felt ridiculously good about it.

The canoe was free, but we still had to get it from one side of this mountain of timber to the other – to the side of the logjam where the river was running through and out of it. We threaded the canoe through the timber dam like a pencil through a bird's nest. First, we got it up on top of the log pile. Next, we carefully slid it along a big-skinned, three-feet-through balsam that ran the length of the entire logjam. Sammy climbed down to near water level, and Jack and I lowered the boat down to him. We tied it off there and rested. Even sitting there exhausted, we could see the canoe was bent in the middle. However, after surveying it from all angles, Sammy was able to pop the dent out of it.

In our own little way, we were trying to do the same thing as that poor beat-up canoe. We were ready to do whatever it took, to withstand any torture, in order to survive. Freeing Sammy's canoe doesn't sound like much, but to us it was a major accomplishment, a heroic feat of strength and cunning. It felt like, "We finally won one." We were alive, and no one was seriously injured, yet. Until now, we had been as insignificant as pebbles being flushed down stream. We were at the mercy of this river, but we were fighting back in a small way. Freeing the canoe was a morale booster and one small step for an otherwise exhausted, depressed, scared, and disgruntled corps.

So we sat, fatigued, yet proud. Our hands were still stinging from the rope burns, and our muscles ached anew. This last test had required straining different muscles from the ones we'd used up already. From atop the logjam, we saw Gabe across the river and downstream. He looked like he was reaching down to the ground on that little island where he was marooned and picking up something. We tried to figure out what he was doing. Jack guessed he was picking up old baseball caps and flip-flops that had been washed down by the big floods. We couldn't even hear him over the roar from the water. We could see him, and we hoped he was okay until we could reach him.

From atop the logjam, we could see something else, something far more disturbing: a dangerous-looking rapid. It was the first thing we'd face when we got back in our canoes and started back down the river. It was a mean-looking stretch, and then there was a second rapid, where logs and limbs were sticking out from the bank. It looked like a Manganese death trap, the kind where holes are dug and spikes implanted into the ground to kill tigers if they fall in or get too near it. Logs and limbs were jutting out everywhere at just about eye level, right where we'd be coming through. We had three choices. The river split into three sections, and we could take our chances, though none of our choices looked worth a spit.

On the right-hand side, just about where our faces would be, were big, jagged logs. Forget that one. Our next option, the center, appeared to be a good choice. But right in the center of the river was a huge slab rock between two other large boulders where the water narrowed and gushed over and around it. We couldn't see downstream below the roaring whitewater, which meant there was a waterfall where the river just dropped off below the big rock. We wanted no part of that.

Our only option was to run the section to our left, but it would be fast—a real nasty-looking stretch, definitely a class 1V rapid, maybe a class V1, I don't know. In this rapid, the whitewater went on for forty-to-sixty yards, and these weren't just whitecaps; most of the river was white and foaming. That's what we faced: exhausted, freezing, shaking, with Sammy bleeding like the proverbial stuck pig from the gash above his left eye.

Picking up Gabe was going to be another problem. It was going to be difficult to cross to the other side of the river so quickly after we started. He was too close. We couldn't just paddle over to him because the current was too strong. We decided that Jack would ride with me, and we would paddle back up river, cross over, and pick up Gabe in our canoe. Once we got Gabe in the boat, we'd try to meet Sammy after he shot around the logjam rapid alone. Then, he'd try and stop before he hit the Big Nasty rapid downstream. We didn't want Sammy to go through the rapid with no one in his canoe, and we didn't want to try it with three in ours. It would be disastrous.

There were some willows at the toe of the island where Gabe was marooned. If we were lucky, we could pull in there and make the switch, and Gabe could get back into Sammy's canoe. The only chance we had was going through the Big Nasty with two in each canoe. Well, that was the plan, and it would have worked if only we had gotten a chance to try it. Instead, as soon as Jack and I picked up Gabe, somehow the canoe overturned. Next thing we knew, both Gabe and Jack were underneath the boat and underwater. Gabe was fighting to get back up to the surface, but Jack was between him and air. They tussled like two cats in a barrel under water until they both jerked their heads up for air.

Our carefully worked-out strategy was all shot to hell. Now we were all loose from our canoes, floating wildly at enormous speeds downriver again. It happened so quick I don't even know how we got back into the canoe or got ready for the upcoming rapid. I don't know what happened next or how. All I can remember is somehow Sammy picked up Gabe. Jack got back into my canoe. But, I don't have any idea how that happened.

We were flying, now. We were heading downriver fast. Jack and I thought we were in a pretty good position to withstand the treacherous, long rapid we'd been calling the Big Nasty. But this was the first time Jack showed any sign of fear, and when he did, it completely unnerved me. Not because I felt that Jack shouldn't be afraid, but because I had gotten him into this mess, and I couldn't do anything more than this flimsy effort to get him out of it.

"If anything happens to him. . . ." It was that horrible thought. I just couldn't imagine it. Then, my thinking was interrupted by Jack saying, "Dad, we're not going to make it!" It was more like he screamed it. Me? I was thinking, "I know that." The scary thing was that I knew he was right. But I said, "We'll make it!"

I lied, I guess. We were riding a curl down the middle of the river like on a surfboard. As we did, huge swells cut into the sides of our canoe. They were bombarding us like we were in the North Atlantic on a bad day. Jack was screaming, "No we're not! No we're not!!"

We ran that rapid about as good as it could be run. It didn't matter. We sank anyway. Now it was asses and elbows all the way down again in the fierce, furious water. I struggled to reach the surface and get a gulp of air. I couldn't! When I finally got my head above water and tried to breath, a wave hit me, and another. I took in a mouthful of water before making it to the surface.

I was heading downriver out of control, face first. All I could think about was Lynnie and not bringing our Jack home with me. Where was he? God, I was scared, mostly for Jack and his mother. What a horrible, horrid thought. Get it out of your mind. Forget "Where's Jack? You'd better save yourself!" is what I was thinking as I tumbled down that river. "You can't do anything for him right now, just keep yourself alive. Don't drown; it's all you can do for Jack right now."

Where was Jack? I finally saw him tumbling behind me. He looked okay. He was floating like a top, his life-jacket keeping him up on the surface. We all had life-jackets on. We'd needed them all day, and we definitely needed them now. We spun and spurted and rolled I don't know how far down that river. We banged into rocks. "Ow!" We rammed into boulders, reached and grabbed at anything, trying to latch onto something to stop us. Round, moss-covered boulders went flying by as we literally zoomed downriver with our butts up, until finally I could swing my legs around and, at least, get my feet in front of me.

Most of the time I peddled furiously underwater with my legs, trying to keep my head back and my butt up, going down feet first. As I did, I could feel the rocks on the bottom of the river hit my bottom. I remember thinking how smooth they were. But it was scary, as I thought how easily my feet could get lodged in the boulder pile lining the bottom of the river.

I was going through bushes, brushing by sticks of some kind. No, it was a tree limb. Trees! Oh, Jeez! I was caught, caught in the crook of a large tree. The power of the water was pinning me there, wouldn't let me go. I arched backwards so the force of the water couldn't pin me up against this tree. As I did, the water just rolled me up and over the tree limb. It ripped my shirt and scraped my back. Argh! More pain! I was free floating again. "Get my feet up," I was telling myself. "Lie on your back, butt up!" I had no idea where our canoe was and didn't care. It was gone. Jack and I ended up holding onto the bank.

We had gone through the Big Nasty first. Now it was Sammy and Gabe's turn. They started from just past the logjam and saw what happened to us. We'd tried to make it over to the left shoot but couldn't get there. That's what Sammy and Gabe tried to do, too. They didn't make it either. They got about half way and ended up shooting downstream between the two big boulders in the middle of the river and getting hung out to dry over the big flat rock.

Sammy said later the rock was almost above the water line, but that the force of the river was so powerful it didn't matter. When they hit it and scraped the bottom of their canoe, it thrust them out clear over the edge. Gabe, being in the front of the canoe, was suspended in space like in some crazy kind of Road-runner cartoon. Below him was a drop of nearly four feet to the churning water. It was bizarre looking. Jack and I couldn't believe what we were seeing.

The rock caused the canoe to skid to a complete stop. They couldn't back up, as the force of the river was incredible. Yelling at Gabe to hang on, Sammy remained there suspended in the air, both of them still in their canoe, for about five seconds. Then, just as they finished surveying their situation, they looked at each other with goofy, quizzical expressions and braced themselves for the crash. That's when the canoe eventually gave up the ghost and hit the boiling water below. Boom! As it did, they did, too.

Sammy remembers being upright in the canoe, when all of a sudden, the canoe abruptly slowed. Then, it stopped, with the river gurgling below and raging all around them. Their canoe backed up, actually went backwards! Sammy realized he was caught in a hydraulic; there was nothing he could do.

When the canoe began to back up, the water began to pour into the canoe's stern. The more water they took in, the deeper it sank, until Sammy was waist deep, though still standing in the boat with his arms half extended. Then, the boat hit the bottom and ricocheted back up, the river spitting out the canoe like a splinter from an infected finger. It shot the canoe free but without Sammy and Gabe. They were flying free once again, hauling ass downriver.

During this particular spill, Gabe actually did get his foot caught. It could have been catastrophic. As he was being washed downriver, his ankle got caught between two rocks. Quickly, using all of his strength, Gabe somehow managed to cling to a low hanging limb that unbelievably just appeared above him. With his strength, he was able to get both hands up to the tree limb and pull himself loose. He was lucky; we were all lucky.

Gabe didn't say much during most of this experience. He said nothing at all about fear to me during the entire ordeal, nor did he express anything of the kind to Jack. I'm not sure the subject ever came up between them. Throughout this entire adventure, these young men, ages fifteen and sixteen, were amazingly calm, helpful, sturdy and brave. Their behavior put Sammy and me to shame for getting them into this situation in the first place.

Often since, I've thought about how close we came to drowning during this river adventure. I'm not exaggerating the fear, danger, and shock we experienced during this near-death experience, for that is what it was: near death. I know that sounds crazy, because if we had been thinking clearly we wouldn't have gotten ourselves in such a dangerous situation in the first place.

Though we didn't know it at the time, I believe all of us were in shock from this point on. What had happened up until now was reactionary. It involved our instinct to survive, and things happened extremely fast. We never stopped or slowed down; we were continuously moving. We were constantly flying through the whitewater, dumping water from our canoes, trying to right or even find our boats. We were always reacting to forces beyond our control.

Except for sitting down and resting after we freed Sammy's canoe from the logjam, we didn't stop moving the entire trip. It was all very basic, primordial. We had all been in whitewater before: on the Ocoee, Nantahala, Big South Fork, and many other rivers. But nothing we'd ever experienced in those rivers was anything like what happened to us on Abrams Creek. We could very easily have been killed. It was purely by the hand of God that we weren't.

Originally, at the time of this adventure, I had attributed our survival to fate, luck, anything to explain it. There had to be a reason at least one of us didn't drown or sustain a serious injury. Through the grace of God and through none of our own efforts, we made it. I don't know how to explain it other than it was the hand of providence that saved us.

No Hikers Paradise

At this point everything changed. In a sense, it was a "heart of darkness" kind of experience. Sammy's red canoe was spinning like buttered corn in a soap dish downriver. We saw it float away, hundreds of yards ahead of us until it went around a bend and out of sight. In fact, both boats were gone, along with all our gear, our food, our fishing poles, everything. All we had left was the proverbial clothes on our backs.

But we were alive, all of us, standing on terra firma, DRY GROUND. It was good to be close to Sammy and Gabe and Jack again. We were together, undivided. Somehow we felt safer when we were close to each other. Whew! We stood around grinning and looking at one another with opossum-looking smiles on our faces. We were a pretty motley beat-up crew, all shivering uncontrollably from the cold. Sammy looked the worst. The cut over his eye was open, but it wasn't bleeding as bad as it had been earlier. The cold water had cleaned him up some, washed all the blood off his face. Still, he looked like hell. We all looked like hell.

As near as we could figure out, our location wasn't good. We were on the left bank, the left-hand side of the river about a mile-and-a half downstream from the logjam. We were five or six miles downriver from where we started. "What are we going to do now?" was the question on everybody's mind. We could see we were in a steep gorge deep in the heart of the Great Smoky Mountains. It was something like a canyon. We were completely surrounded by steep walls, bluffs hundreds of feet high. It was like we were inside a bowl or a giant bucket.

The left side of the river was the wrong side to be on. There was no path, no trail on this side. We knew it, but there was no way we could make it back across that raging river. To try would be pushing our luck. We'd been in the water for about six hours. We were freezing and weak. But we sure were ready to walk. There wasn't anything else we could do. So we started to climb out.

We knew there was a pretty good possibility we wouldn't make it out that night. I remember thinking about how happy I was, what a good stroke of luck I had three Bic lighters with me. We were going to need them later. I had pockets all over me. I was wearing my vest, shirt, and jeans. After trying my pockets and not finding any lighters, I gave up because my finger hurt too much to be digging around in wet, tight areas. I'll get them later, I thought. Anyway, Sammy said he had a lighter.

So, there was nothing to do but try to keep the river on our right and climb out. It couldn't be any farther than a couple of miles. Our destination was the mouth of Abrams Creek where it intersects Highway 129 at the bridge by Chilhowee Lake. We were heading right to where we had parked our car. Our assignment was simple: follow the river to the lake and get out, safely.

We climbed up to the top of the ridge and started walking. Climbing was tricky because it was so steep. The land was so up-tilted it almost rubbed your nose as you walked or climbed. Like they say, it was "steep as a mule's face." At first, we were excited about walking and climbing, about just being on land. Anything was better than that damn river which had treated us so brutally. So far there hadn't been much to enjoy on the Great River Adventure, but I guarantee you we enjoyed ourselves when we first started to climb out of there on real dirt.

We were all grateful to be alive. In fact, we were plumb happy about it, even joyous. We weren't exactly singing, but it sure was good to see four scrambling butts working their way up the mountainside on good ole mother earth. Whatever else was going to happen from here on out on this crazy adventure, at least we weren't going to drown.

When we first started walking, we began to warm because of the terrain. We figured we were hypothermic. We had been so cold for so long. We weren't quite sure what hypothermic was exactly, because none of us had ever experienced it. But, we knew it had something to do with getting dangerously cold and not being able to get warm. It pretty well described Sammy's condition. He was in the worst shape. He just couldn't stop shaking.

All of our clothes were wet: jeans, tennis shoes, and life jackets. Jack had on an all-weather coat under his life jacket, a long-sleeved shirt, and hiking boots. I had on jeans and a long-sleeved shirt under my life jacket. Sammy was dressed like Burt Reynolds in the movie *Deliverance* – shirtless under his life jacket, which he wore like a vest. With his scraggly beard, he looked just as rugged, too. Gabe wore a tee shirt and knee-length hiking shorts. This certainly was no country to walk through in shorts. However, there was nothing any of us could do about what we were wearing or not wearing.

We were in a different world now. It was a world of dirt, dappled sunlight, and plants – solid things – and it felt good (see Plate 24). Anything was better than being in the amorphous liquid world of cold and endless water. We were scrambling, zigzagging back and forth, up the ridge. Even so, it was a struggle getting through dog hobble, and past the thirty-five foot high giant rhododendrons, which lined the first fifty yards up the side of the gorge from the creek.

We thought if we could get above the rhododendrons, certainly there would be a trail. At least, the terrain would get better, and then it would be easier traveling. But when we finally got above them, the joke was on us. There was no trail or anything like one. Further, we couldn't see the river, which was now below us, although we could still hear it.

We weren't hiking, and we weren't actually even walking. It was more like scrambling, climbing on all fours like mountain goats, jumping around from a rhododendron branch to a small beech tree to a rock which might or might not withstand our weight. Again and again, back and forth, this is the way we worked our way up the steep banks, which were eight-hundred to a thousand feet in some places. Our entire world consisted of how to move, where to put our hands, where to put each foot. These were our only concerns for what seemed like hours.

Wearing tennis shoes had been a good idea on the river, where one is washed around like clothes in a washer or bashed against rocks. But, on this terrain, they weren't as useful. They quickly filled with loamy dirt as small avalanches of black earth tumbled down and covered our feet to the shins. We were breaking and kicking loose virgin earth that may not have been trampled on for over one-hundred years—maybe never. No Native American in his right mind would walk through here.

We tried to veer west as we worked our way up the steep gorge at a forty-five-degree angle. Traveling at an angle worked much better than trying to climb vertically. Little things became big things in this world: "Ah, there's a nice place for me to put my feet! I like that. It'll hold me." Or, "That's where Sammy stepped. I think I'll try that."

Sammy was in the lead, then Jack, then me, while Gabe brought up the rear. The river running through this country snakes back and forth. Our plan was simple: keep the river on our right, follow Abrams Creek. Eventually, the creek will flow into Chilhowee Lake, and we'll come to a slew, a settling lagoon about a mile-and-a-half before the Highway 129 bridge at the lake. That is our destination. Sooner or later we'll end up there.

We continued heading west, keeping the river on our right. We just walked and walked and walked, occasionally looking up at the ridges, which all looked the same. Sammy traveled effortlessly, moving through the forest like a Native American. He always seemed to be twenty or thirty yards ahead of us. Jack called him "Tracker Joe." Sometimes, we could barely make him out. He was just a flash, moving amongst hemlock leaves, rhododendron, and laurel. Sammy moved on, and we followed—tired, bruised, exhausted, and beat up.

As we hiked, the river wound around and through one of the ridges. But we couldn't always tell which one for sure. This meant there was no short cutting around anything. We had to stay above the creek, no matter what type of rough terrain we were traversing. There was just no easy way. We continued to bushwhack our way, breaking new trail everywhere we went.

When we came to where the ridgeline descended, we traveled it and went where it led. When it went down, we knew that meant it would be going back up. The constant climbing was not only exhausting, but it was also demoralizing. We'd been rejuvenated for a short time by getting off the river. Now we were getting acclimated to a completely different type of physical torture. Welcome to the Great Smoky Mountains wilderness of five-hundred-thousand acres of forested lands where people get lost regularly. Some are never heard from again!

Luckily for us, most of the leaves, briars, and poison vines hadn't regenerated yet. Plants, trees, and overgrowth were only sprouting their seasonal foliage. But don't kid yourself; there were plenty of briars everywhere we traveled. We could see through the forest about as far as twenty or thirty yards ahead of us. In some places, where the canopy was completely full, we couldn't see the sky. The way forward was full of huge hemlocks, white pines, maples, poplars, red oaks and white oaks, all wearing spring foliage.

It would have been much worse for us if the under-story had been thicker. It would have been much more difficult, for instance, to move through this forest later in the season, and in the summer it would have been nearly impossible. In this sense, we were lucky.

Following the ridgeline was the easiest way to travel, although we still had to go up and down along the spine of the mountains as the terrain dictated. Gabe, in his shorts, was always falling back. He spent much of his time pulling briars out of his knees. He couldn't travel as fast as the rest of us who wore jeans. Stretches of neck-deep briars, dog hobble, cat briars, and Hercules club were common. It seemed they all scratched, cut, and tore. So, Sammy, Jack, and I made as big a trail through the virgin country as we could. It was like following somebody walking through deep snow. Each person broke trail for the one behind him. In this way, we tried to help Gabe and provide him some relief. But, it barely showed. Within an hour his legs looked like he'd been whipped with a cat-a-nine-tails. We cringed when we stopped and Gabe showed them to us. His legs were ripped to shreds. The greatest relief was a fallen pine. It gave us an easy forty to sixty feet of good trail. We scampered along it like squirrels and used its limbs to keep our balance. This was no hiker's paradise.

We built up a manageable trail speed through these woods. We wanted desperately to get home that night. This country was black bear terrain and European wild boar habitat. If there were panthers, this is where they would live. And they'd be here if they could find something to eat, like us. Yikes!

Ultimately, we knew the only way to get through was to move like a tank and just rip our way through. So we did. We were as agile as we could be, positioning ourselves to avoid briars and everything else that might catch or latch onto us. Because of the terrible floods and recent winter ice storms, big holes existed through the forest canopy, ripped open by fallen timber. Huge blackberry patches were common in these areas, briar traps created when big holes in the canopy opened and the light got through.

For what seemed like hours we moved up one ridge and down the other, jumping over trickles, brooks, and side branches flowing into Abrams Creek (see Plate 26). We'd rock-hop a shallow trickle and move back and forth up the side of a ridge like a logging train on a switch-back. Then we'd go down again. Up, up, we'd climb on the opposite ridge from where we'd just crossed the brook. We'd end up on the other side of the same mountain and across the creek from where we'd just been. Then, we'd cross over a ridge, come to another sloped ridge leading to a creek and do it all over again. Maybe this time, if we were lucky, we'd walk the ridgeline for a while where it was more level.

All the while, we watched the sun continue to set. This worried us more than anything, because it appeared like the sun was moving. It freaked us out. It couldn't be! We couldn't figure it out. We could still hear the river—we'd worked hard to always keep the river on our right, a conscious decision to keep us from getting lost. We just had to follow Abrams Creek. So, we couldn't be lost. Or were we?

Eventually, we discovered that we had actually traveled in a circle. "Hey, we walked this ridge an hour ago," Sammy hollered out. Tired after having walked as far as we had, this was frustrating and scary news. It was a terribly lonely, disappointing, and depressing feeling to discover we'd made no progress. How could this be? Sammy and I just couldn't figure out what was going on. All these damn ridges looked the same.

We'd just lost another hour of daylight—daylight we couldn't afford to spare. As the sun went down, it was getting colder. This was the gloaming time, the period in the day around dusk when the spirits come out and the Scotsman's pipes fill the misty air of the Smoky Mountains. Here we were, still in the woods with less and less of a chance of getting out before nightfall.

All along, Jack insisted we walk along the riverbank. "Let's go down. Let's go down and walk by the river," he kept saying.

And I kept saying, "Jack, we can't walk by the river. There's no trail down there. We can't get through down there."

"There isn't any trail here either," was his comeback, and he was right. Finally, exhausted and confused, we stopped walking. While Sammy, Jack, and Gabe flopped to the ground, I volunteered to go ahead and scout the location of the creek/river to make sure it was really there. "Let the boys rest," I thought. "I got them in here; at least I can try a little harder to get them out. I'll do this. I can do this! It's strictly physical. That's okay, I like walking, hiking, breaking trail. This is the least I can do." This is the way I was thinking as I searched for the creek.

It was easy dropping down the hillside—it always is. It's getting back up on the other side that's the hard part. The closer I got down toward the river, the more fear and disappointment gripped me. It didn't matter anyway because what I found when I finally got to the bottom of that ridge was a good-sized creek, but it wasn't Abrams Creek. It was a creek only a quarter of the size of Abrams Creek. The reality set in. We'd slipped down a side branch and were lost again. "Shit!"

Sammy's face dropped to the ground when I told him. Quickly thinking about our next move, his face regained its fairly stoic nature. I told the boys about our latest situation. They didn't care, or if they did, they didn't let on. They were just too tired for it to register. "C'mon! Get up! We've got to go down and find the creek again. We're off on a side branch. Get up. Get up!" We had to rouse them like we were in the army. They looked as if they could sleep right there in their wet clothes, in a big heap of sweat, briars, and mud.

In no time we were all hopping rocks again, crossing the little creek. It was lush and beautiful down there, with more rhododendrons and a good-looking trout stream. It was like a lost world (see Plate 25). However, we didn't have the time or inclination to do anything but look. We had to worry about going back down the creek and retracing our steps. We made pretty good time, too. Finally, we made it back to Abrams Creek, the real Abrams Creek this time.

As we traveled through the forest, we noticed passing indentations in the earth, which appeared to be animal beds. They looked like downed brush and shrubs, surrounded by five to eight feet of sunken, beat-down underbrush. These beds usually had leaves and soft earth beaten, loosened up, and worked in around them. They looked like something a bear, a deer, or other large animal used to bed down in. We thought we might be doing this same thing ourselves soon enough. We just hoped we wouldn't freeze to death doing it.

It was still daylight, so we walked on. We saw another of these animal beds and thought it might be our best chance for a decent campsite. But it was too early. There was still some light left, so we passed it up and pressed on. Onward and upward and downward and upward until, finally, we came to a rock face in the mountain with a sheer rock bluff above it, forty to sixty feet high. It was impossible to see the top of the mountain above us from where we were.

We were right next to it; a nice Native American rock shelter is what it looked like – a shallow cave opening at the base of a rock cliff. The roof was five- or six-feet high. It was long and wide enough for all of us to crawl inside. Native American rock shelters have always fascinated me, and immediately I began kicking around dry earth and dust from the ground, until Jack shouted out, "Hey! We don't have time to hunt for arrowheads." Of course, he was right.

We turned and looked up high above us at this new ridge we had to climb, this new mountain. Whew! We looked at one another, and though we ached and our entire bodies were stiffening up from head to toe from this ordeal, we had no choice. So we started up again, up, up, up, climbing yet another damn mountain, now bone tired and cold. In spite of the rough physical exertion of climbing yet another ridge, we could feel it getting colder and colder. When we stopped briefly to get our bearings, to find the best route for the next twenty or thirty feet, we could feel the chill in the wind as it made contact with our sweat.

It was nearly dark by the time we made it to the top of this ridge. Pushing through the thick brush was becoming harder.

We were losing daylight. But one thing gave us hope, one good thought kept running through my head: "Sammy has a Bic lighter. Sammy has a Bic lighter!" It was true. I knew it. I heard him say it. He did say it, didn't he? Yeah.

"Sammy!" I called out. "Yeah," he said. "You have a Bic lighter, right?"

"Yeah," Sammy said. "Yeah," I thought, "Sammy's got a Bic lighter. Good!"

Finally, atop the ridge, we picked the first open knoll. We were exhausted and ready to flop. "We're going to need firewood, lots of firewood," Sammy said. The boys were still flopping, destroyed, half-dead, still lying on the ground. I was moving like a robot, myself. If I stopped doing it, I was afraid it was over. I was done—I might die! That's how bad I felt. Everything ached at once.

The wind whistled through this campsite, and it bothered all of us. I was worried about how cold it was going to get later that night. Meanwhile, I was wandering in the woods, twenty or thirty feet away, looking half-heartedly for firewood, when I came upon it. "Hey! Here's one of those deer beds! Let's sleep here. C'mon."

So we found a deer bed, a knoll, not quite atop the ridge, but sitting just below it where we'd be out of the wind. It was nestled in a depression about eight feet across, obviously a recently used animal bed. There were crumpled leaves, surrounded by five or six large trees, three and four feet through. The ground was soft and sunken below the surrounding ground, like a small pit. It was just big enough for the four of us. The trees rimmed the corners of the area and offered some protection from the wind. Their dead limbs would provide plenty of firewood, as well. It was an ideal spot. I wouldn't call it a campsite, but it was the best we could do.

I thought to myself, "If we didn't get a fire going soon, we were going to be in real trouble. Not only will we actually freeze to death, but we also need the light from the fire to find firewood!" But wait a minute! This was crazy talk. It didn't make any sense at all. Because if we couldn't get a fire going, we wouldn't need any firewood, knucklehead! With thoughts like these, I could tell my mind was starting to fog up. I think I was hypothermic.

But, it's actually pretty damn interesting, fascinating in fact, to realize your thinking is not right. It's actually a little bit scary, too. And that's what happened: we actually came to a point where we recognized our minds were playing tricks on us. We were becoming more of a threat to our own wellbeing, making decisions that might actually put ourselves in harm's way. We were our own greatest threat out there.

I was bone tired. Sammy looked haggard, worried, and freezing. He was the coldest one amongst us. Meanwhile, the boys hadn't said a word. They didn't complain about anything. Lying there, the boys were like zombies. "Huh . . . wood? Yeah . . . wood!" Gabe would say. "Wood, Gabe," Jack would say, and he'd stagger around, maybe come back with a switch or two. I don't know how long he thought a switch would burn, maybe a minute. There did, however, appear to be plenty of dead wood, fallen trees, and firewood everywhere close by. We couldn't see because it was dark. In the land of the noonday sun, the sun had gone behind the mountains. It had gotten pitch dark on us phenomenally quickly, in mere moments.

About this time, we remembered we were due back in Knoxville any minute. In fact, we were late and going to be a lot later. Oh, man, I thought. I don't need to be thinking about my wife Lynnie, Jack's poor mother. It's the last thing I need to be worrying about, because I can't do anything about it. We told the wives we'd be home before dark. They knew that meant we'd be home at dark or later. Hopefully, they're not worrying unnecessarily yet. There will be plenty of time later on tonight when they'll worry necessarily!

Turning to Sammy for reassurance, I said, "Maybe Theresa and Lynnie aren't worrying about us yet? What do you think, Sammy?"

"Ah, they probably figure we're just out late again. Every time we go out like this, something happens. They know that. They're not stupid. Forget it, they're not worried yet."

Sammy had his Bic lighter out of his pocket. I couldn't find mine. Frantically, I was searching for it. However, my hand, especially my ring finger, was so sore I couldn't get my swollen hand into my pocket. My jeans were wet and muddy and clinging to me like saran wrap. I couldn't do it. I knew I had at least three lighters somewhere in my pockets. I tried my vest pockets, shirt pockets, even the back of my fishing vest. It had holes in the vest pockets and no seam, so stuff migrates around to my back where it hides from me. But when I checked, I didn't find any lighter. Nada, damn it! I was sure I had three lighters this morning for just this type of emergency.

Meanwhile, Jack and Gabe were shielding Sammy's hands from the wind. Sammy had his lighter, and he was flicking it again and again. Oh God! Nothing was happening. Not even a spark. Sammy was shaking terribly. No wonder it wouldn't light. He kept trying and blowing on the lighter between flicks, trying to dry it out, but with no luck. Flick . . . flick . . . flick . . . nothing.

Sammy was so cold his hands were jumping six inches from side to side each time he shook. He was jerking, just about in convulsions. I kept thinking, "Give me the damn lighter, I'll make it light. Where's my lighter? Dad gum it!"

"Blow on it! Here, let me try," said Jack.

"Let me try it, Sammy!" I was pleading. We were grabbing for his lighter. Gabe, it looked like, was walking around in circles. I don't know what Gabe was doing. He was just turning round and round in a circle like dogs sometimes do. It was some kind of a shortened version of pacing. He was probably just trying to keep warm.

At the exact same time this was happening, another conversation was taking place back home in Knoxville. "Hi Lynn, this is Suzanne Gagliardi." The phone didn't have to ring more than twice. Lynnie was expecting a call, though she was expecting it from me. She was expecting me to call and tell her the usual: "Sammy and I are all right. We're just a little late. We're on our way home." Instead, it was a woman's voice, Gabe's mother, and she wasn't used to the way Sammy and I were always late when we went on an adventure. In fact, she didn't even know Sammy. She was worried, of course, because Gabe wasn't home and it was getting late. She asked, "Have you heard from the boys, Lynn?"

All Lynnie could say was she hadn't heard from us. "Probably they stopped for dinner or something and are just running late. Don't worry."

Suzanne then said, "Lynn, I have a bad feeling about this. I think we should call someone."

"No, let's wait a little while longer. I'm sure they're fine," Lynnie said.

Suzanne Gagliardi waited until ten o'clock then called back to say, "I want to get somebody out there looking for them." So Lynn called Theresa Tillery and asked her if she had heard from Sammy. By eleven thirty, Theresa had called Andy – a real woods pro and friend of Sammy's and mine. Andy and his friend Robert had guided us down the Big South Fork River before, more than once. Andy volunteered to search for us if we didn't turn up. But he was confident we would sooner or later.

This was little consolation to Theresa or Suzanne or Lynn. Theresa thanked Andy and told him she would call as soon as we got back or if she needed him in the morning. Then, after conferring again with Suzanne and Lynn, she called her friend Hal to get the emergency number for the Great Smoky Mountains National Park. Theresa, Lynn, and Suzanne gave descriptions of us to the rangers in the hope they would find us. They described what we looked like, what we were wearing, when and where we were last seen, what our vehicles looked like, our canoes, and even the equipment we were using. They gave this information to Park Ranger Mike Farley, the ranger stationed at the Abrams Creek Campground.

Ranger Farley reassured our families that "This kind of thing occurs often, regularly." He also informed the ladies that searchers were already out looking for us at the few locations where there was access. They had found our cars where we'd left them, but there was no sign of us. He spent a good portion of that Saturday night in contact with Lynn, Theresa, and Suzanne, trying to help them through this difficult time. He promised that, "By first light, we will have men in the woods."

Another serendipitous turn of events was also occurring. It turned out Jack had promised a friend of ours, Roger Clapp, Jack's Sunday-school teacher, that he would help edit a video-tape project for Sunday school. It was due Sunday, the next day. So, Roger came over at nine p.m. on Saturday night to help Jack with the project. Jack, of course, wasn't home, and neither was I, and nobody knew when we would be. But Roger was good enough to stay during the ordeal until very late to assist with the search by phone and to support Lynn.

Back on the ridge, we were trying to assemble as much wood as we could. We knew it might not last half the night, but it was a start. But we still couldn't get the lighter to work. Flick - nothing. Flick - nothing. Flick . . . flick . . . flick. I grabbed the lighter. I couldn't stand it anymore. I blew on it. It wasn't wet. So, I flicked it, fully expecting it to light. It didn't. I couldn't understand it. Sammy grabbed it back from me and tried again. He flicked it. Nothing happened. He flicked it again. Whoa! This time it sparked!

I don't know how many times Sammy flicked that Bic. But after about seventy-five flicks, it finally lit. It did, praise God! Sammy moved a single dry leaf very slowly just above the tiny lighter. He gently lowered the dry leaf, easing it ever so slightly and carefully down to just above the lighter. It caught fire. It lit and was burning. The leaf was actually burning: Halleluiah!

Carefully, slowly, with both hands, one holding the leaf and the other the lighter, Sammy set the half-burning leaf down and put a pine needle on top of it. I put a third leaf on it. My leaf was actually two strands of a loblolly pine needle, the size of a bobby pin. But it burned, too. Jack and Gabe put leaves on it. We had fire.

We were freezing, and instantly we could feel the sacred warmth from our tiny fire, no bigger than an ashtray burning. Yet it seemed like it warmed the entire forest. We were very careful. Only single leaves, only toothpick-sized wood at first. Then, gradually we started putting tiny shards of dead wood on the fire. Finally, dry twigs from limbs that snapped when you touched them.

Ah, we enjoyed putting bigger wood on our fire. In no time, we were busting dead pine logs across giant fallen trees. Logs were spinning and flying through the air like in *2001: A Space Odyssey*. All manner of carbon was being heaved from the darkness upon our fire. We gathered wood like manna from heaven, as if it were a prayer or celebration. The bigger our fire, the more animated, and excited we became. We almost danced around it.

Out of the darkness, sparks flew upwards into the air above

the trees. The light show reverberated throughout the firmament. Each time we neared the fire and dropped our load, we received wonderful, beautiful, radiant heat for our efforts. We had to force ourselves to back away from the fire into the darkness and go hunt for more wood. Everything was going to be all right. We had a fire.

By the time we all gathered in the center around the fire, we were breathing heavily, but we had warmed ourselves and accumulated a fair-sized pile of wood. We had a pile three-feet high and four-feet long, but it still wasn't enough firewood for the night. Sammy went to sleep instantly. I never saw anything like it. One moment we were all standing in front of our fire, like animals over a kill; the next, Sammy was dead asleep. He was out cold – way too near the fire and with no shirt under his wet vest. He was curled up in a fetal position eight inches from the edge of our fire. It looked like his hair was smoking!

We tapered the fire down to a more practical size, in order to save our precious wood. I kept thinking about the old energy conservation tale I learned while working for TVA. It compares the white man's misuse of fuel and poor energy conservation to the Native American's use. It goes something like "the white man built great big fires and stood way back from them, while Native Americans built a small fire and sat right up next to it to keep warm, using much less fuel." We began to move in closer and sit right up next to a smaller, hotter fire.

We also started to think more clearly, it seemed. I don't know if this is actually true or not, but I believe it is. We began to gain control over our faculties again and were less manic. There was no longer panic in our thoughts and in everything we did. For the first time in nearly twelve hours, we felt warm. Our clothes were still wet, but sitting there by the fire was the closest thing we had come to being comfortable and safe in a long day of fear, chaos, and danger. It felt good.

Sammy was lying dead asleep, curled up with his head uphill just to the left of the fire. We didn't have to worry about all 130 pounds of frozen Sammy taking up too much space by the fire. He was curled up so tightly he only took up about two square feet. He was still wet. But we didn't think it would do any good to try to wake him and get him out of his wet clothes. He was sleeping too soundly, like a brick. So we let him sleep wet clothes and all. He needed to get warm and stay warm. He was exhausted.

"Ole Tracker Joe" got us here, nearly halfway out as best we could figure. He did it by walking twenty to thirty yards ahead of the rest of us most of the afternoon. He looked like a character from a jungle movie or out of *Green Mansions* or someone from *The Heart of Darkness*. He really does resemble the real Jesse James—with that one eye of his about half-cocked, especially standing there in the deep woods of the forest studying what nature has presented him.

Sammy is "a good hand in the woods," as they say. He and his brother, Jimmy, learned a great deal from their father about hunting and fishing in the woods around Norris, Tennessee. Sammy is as good a friend as I've got. If I ever had to be in a situation like this again, Sammy's the guy I'd want to be with.

I continued hunting and gathering wood in the darkness and gradually worked further and further out from the light of our camp. Dead wood was everywhere. Giant fallen trees stretched across the entrance to our camp. We used one of them, the biggest, as our busting log. We'd hold on to one end and throw or swing it against that dry, dead, fallen log. In this manner, we were able to collect and store half-a-cord of wood, including logs two-feet thick and four-feet long. We knew we needed them for the cold night ahead. "Twice warmed," as the saying goes. We were warmed once while getting it, and again when we burned it.

Warmth covered us amidst the solitude and the soft sounds emitting from the fire. While Sammy slept, Gabe, Jack, and I quietly talked in the darkness of the Great Smoky Mountains. My hand was so swollen now my wedding ring wouldn't spin at all. I couldn't get it off. But my finger pain was overshadowed by the pain coming from every other nerve and muscle in my body.

Gabe and Jack fell quiet. They started drying their clothes across a stack of wood. Jack's jacket, which he was smart enough to wear, came off first. Shirts, shoes, and socks followed. As we warmed and felt better about our plight, more of our wet clothing came off, and we draped them across the logs scattered around. Our little campsite was full. Clockwise around the fire, Sammy

Plate 19. Abram's Creek runs with snow runoff

Plate 20. Abram's Creek foot bridge near flood stage

Plate 21. Abram's Creek showing steep deep banks

Plate 22. Bald eagle watching as we try to keep from drowning

Plate 23. Example of typical stream during average flow

Plate 24. Sunlight through trees deep in the Smokies

Plate 25. Lost in a cathedral wilderness

Plate 26. Special beauty of a typical side branch showing the sometimes calm, quiet world of wilderness

Plate 27. Wild Boar

Plate 28. Bear by tree, no doubt watching us pass by

Plate 29. Green mansions surround us

Plate 30. Abram's Creek showing steep gorge taken after 2012 tornado

Plates 31 and 32. (Left) Sammy and I at Jack's wedding in 2005; (right) roommates Gabe and Jack at College of Charleston in 2004, four years after our adventure.

slept at ten o'clock. Jack was at about one o'clock. Gabe lay next to him at three o'clock. The big stack of wood filled the space at six o'clock, and I lay around nine o'clock or so.

Tennis shoes may be the slowest thing to dry on this earth. Blue jeans are second. Neither was ever meant to be wet. Luckily, underwear dries pretty fast. We also learned that nothing on God's earth feels better than putting dry underwear back on four cold butts. It wasn't until Gabe and Jack fell asleep that my underwear actually dried. It felt kind of weird, sitting there with my naked butt on dried leaves while the fire sputtered and everybody else snored away.

Our camp looked like a Laundromat. Clothes were slung everywhere in a fairly haphazard manner. Underwear hung high on a three-log teepee. We were all so exhausted that, as soon as we warmed even the tiniest little bit, we dozed off immediately. Until then, we worked hard to keep sparks from igniting and burning up our clothes. But we didn't do a good job of saving all of our stuff.

Shoelaces were the first to catch fire. It wasn't long before the smell of burnt rubber from tennis shoes was in the air. Sparks occasionally kicked out and landed on a shirt. While everyone slept, I acted as Fire Marshall for a while. Using a stick, I reached across and scraped burning embers off our tennis shoes. The shoelaces burned two inches before I was able to put them out.

It was like this for most of the night. All I know is I worked the fire to try to keep it going most of the night, so we could stay warm and dry our clothes. I tried not to get it hot enough to singe the hide of my three buddies. We surrounded that fire like four hot dogs at a picnic. Our backs and backsides would get nice and warm and comfortable, but our faces were freezing. We'd flip over, and the opposite would occur. This went on all night long. Fry on one side. Wake up, put out the fire in your shorts and shoelaces, then roll over and fry a while on the other side. Wake up, throw a log on the fire, and do it all over again. If ever the term *sleeping fitfully* applied to anyone, it applied to us on the ridges of the Great Smoky Mountains that night.

Once, as I was nearly nodding off, I heard a loud rustle from something in the forest behind me. I looked around and called

"Sammy!" in a loud whisper. It startled him, and half-asleep, he sat straight up. Looking through the fire, I saw Gabe staring big-eyed in the same direction. He had heard it, too. "What was that?!" he said, big as life.

"I don't know what it is," I told Gabe. "Maybe it's a 'haint' or a panther," I said, trying to make light of the situation. But, whatever it was, it sounded big and close!

"Maybe it's a deer, moving around out there," I said to Gabe. It was too early in the season for a bear, I thought. They're still hibernating. It might have been a wild hog, though. I'd hate to see one of those beasts tear through our camp while we were all asleep! We got quiet in a hurry and remained absolutely silent for a long while, listening for sounds. The only sound was the fire, which continued to burn. We were quiet and still as death and a bit scared, too. We never heard another noise from whatever critter made the first sound. A couple of hours later, I laid down exhausted with every muscle in my body aching. But at least I was dry, and I finally fell asleep.

"Brrrrr" I was cold. I rolled over twice and was still cold. Sitting up, I saw that the fire had burned down considerably and was about to go out. So, I grabbed a big piece of oak and a few pieces of pine and placed them near a few hot embers, hoping they'd catch, and burn. Using a stick, I poked and twisted the burning logs to spark new life into them. Soon, the fire rekindled, and the guys squirmed back a little. They'd all scooted up near the fire as it had burned down. Now, they all moved back, even while they slept.

It was like a dream as three or four times I awoke and pitched logs onto our fire. Everybody else must have done the same thing as far as I could tell. Late into the night, I remember thinking, "I can't do this again, and I'm not getting up! I'm so tired and warm." My legs and my thighs hurt, and my hand was sore. There was a blister on my thumb. Again, in a smoke-filled, surrealistic dream, I remember seeing Sammy stepping back from the fire into the darkness after dropping more wood. I knew I was not dreaming. This was actually happening. Sammy was up and getting firewood and lots of it. He's probably all right, then, I remember thinking.

A Fisher of Men

A weird clucking sound woke me again. It sounded like "puck, puck, puck." The smell of morning embers and ashes from the mountain of burned firewood engulfed our senses. The misty trickle of the fire's last smoke floated singularly up, twisting and curving above our campfire before it made its way surreptitiously through the canopy. The morning had come, and the mist hung thick over the Great Smoky Mountains.

The world, or what I could see of it, existed only on a horizontal plane. From my pillow, I could see the cool morning mist hanging over everything. My head was resting on something soft. It wasn't actually a pillow, but a bed of leaves on the ground. With eyes open now, I looked out and was aware only of the nature of the world as its smell, sight, and sound touched me sensually.

"Puck, puck, puck." There it was again! What is it? Could it be a turkey? On early mornings like this, certainly every animal in the forest is stirring. We'd been asleep for hours. "Puck, puck, puck." There was a calm persistence in the call now—steady, with a careful, self-assured pause between pucks. It wasn't a turkey. I'd heard that sound before, though, and knew it. My achy body was trying to move, wake up. "Oh!" I was so stiff. I was beginning to lose the soothing womb-like feeling of safety that comes just before waking. Suddenly, just as I became aware of the remembrances and limitations of mortality, the pain set in.

"Yeow!" I screamed when I sat up. At that precise moment, my body began burning as achy feelings busted out everywhere, releasing a huge truckload of pain throughout my body. At the same instant, the "puck" sound went to red alert: "Puck! Puck! PUCK!" it was screaming now, as if letting out a siren call. It kept on and on and on continuously. Whatever was watching us went to screaming, "These invaders to our world, these humans, are ALIVE. Watch out!"

While the "puck, puck, puck" continued screeching throughout the amber misty morning, it soon became clear it was just a flicker, a kind of mountain woodpecker. It wasn't even the giant pileated woodpecker. It sounded like one pissed-off blue jay sounding the neighborhood cat alarm. But this was fierce as anything I've ever heard. It sure was taking our presence personally. The agitated sound woke everyone. A few last logs were thrown on the fire. Sammy began to stretch a bit. Jack and Gabe sat with their knees under their chins, arms wrapped around them while they stared opaquely into the fire. They looked sad, like they couldn't believe they were still in the woods, dumbfounded by a sputtering fire, atop a ridge above a roaring creek—lost somewhere in the Great Smoky Mountains National Park.

Jack and Gabe, under some kind of trance, continued to stare at the fire. They didn't realize it, but while they sat half-awake looking non-plussed, half of all the safety patrol volunteers within a hundred-mile radius, along with a good collection of National Park service employees, were probably out looking for us. If I knew our women correctly, I was certain Lynnie, Theresa, and especially Suzanne Gagliardi had gotten somebody out looking for our butts.

Nothing for breakfast again, after nothing for supper last night. Come to think of it, we didn't have anything for lunch yesterday. No wonder we felt hunger. What we wouldn't give for something to eat, a bath, and especially a cup of coffee. I heard Jack and Gabe talking.

"I dreamed of Shoney's breakfast bar," Jack said.

Gabe added, "Yeah, with piles of bacon . . . pancakes and sausage!"

Jack continued, "All you can eat!" They were laughing maniacally now, as if they'd lost their minds.

"Yeah, they have these real juicy sweet rolls with tons of stuff on them!" said Gabe, and they both laughed and snorted. They sounded like Beavis and Butthead, crazy hungry.

We'd put our last wood on the fire. It gave us enough warmth to try and stand and loosen up our aching muscles and get ready to hike again. None of us were looking forward to it, but we had no other choice. Using a stick, Sammy separated the few logs that were still burning. Kicking and scattering coals, we prepared to leave our place of safety, our place in the forest. Our plan was the same as it had been since getting to dry land. Walk out, keeping the creek on our right. There was nothing else to consider, nothing else we could do to bungle this. Keep it simple, stupid. Keep the creek on your right, you blockhead!

"A helicopter would be nice!" Gabe said to Jack.

"Yeah, they could just drop a rope and haul us out of here."

"Nope, no helicopter's coming." Sammy said.

Jack hollered back to Gabe, "It's the fourth quarter Gabe. It's just like the fourth quarter." Gabe was a football player who played for Farragut. He and Jack both knew it was all guts in the fourth quarter. You've played as hard and as long as you can, but you're not there yet, and there's more work to do. It's when you can't go any more, but you must. When there's no more in the tank. You're running on empty. That was us, all right: running on empty. It fit us to a tee.

I couldn't allow my mind the mysterious pleasure of dwelling on these artificial dreams of rescue. Hope dreams is what they were, trips away from the tortuous and painful reality of the job at hand. We didn't look forward to what we faced, hours and hours of arduous mountain climbing, hiking in the toughest country I've ever seen, and I've moved through some tough places in ten years of shooting video in the Great Smokies. What this day held for us was going to be anything but a walk in the park . . . which it actually was, wasn't it?

"How are we going to put the fire out?" Jack wanted to know as we stood around what little fire remained.

Sammy said, "Jack, you and Gabe are going to help. Get over here; here's how you put a fire out in the woods. You pee on it. That's how you do it." Well, Gabe and Jack were a little shy about helping us put the fire out. Nevertheless, Sammy and I peed on that fire just the same. I always remember as a kid the horrible smell, too, the awful odor produced by peeing on a fire. So, we peed on the fire, a good first-of-the-morning pee, and we nearly put the fire out. We separated the last few hot coals remaining and kicked dirt and ash around the smoldering, stinky embers as best we could. After all, we didn't want to burn the Smokies down. We were going to be in enough trouble with the park rangers as it was.

By the time we started out, we were praying pretty consistently, at least I was. Later, I asked Jack and Gabe if they were as well. "Yeah," they both said, "we were praying." We all kept to ourselves as we started down another endless ridge only to have to climb back up on the other side.

Looking back on it, I suspect this part of the journey was a struggle not to show fear, to show the boys that Sammy and I could get them out of there. We were trying to keep from exhibiting any emotion or say anything that Gabe and Jack might interpret as anything less than a show of strength and confidence. Ha! That's a laugh. But, for some crazy reason, that's just the way it seemed. Maybe the real reason I couldn't share how I really felt was because I was afraid myself. Perhaps I didn't want to admit I was approaching my own last mile-marker. I, too, was in my own fourth quarter. I wasn't sure I could even finish this. But we had no choice.

We walked and hiked and climbed and hiked. The roof of my mouth hurt for some reason. It was painful to swallow. I didn't know what it was. It felt like strep throat. Maybe inhaling all the smoke from the fire had somehow affected my esophagus or larynx, or it might be a sign of dehydration. We hadn't drunk any liquids since we quit drinking involuntarily from Abrams Creek yesterday. We'd been fifteen hours without any water, which is a long time.

"Hey, how you guys feeling?" I managed to holler out, breaking about an hour's silence as we marched through the forest. It was like a forced death march on Bataan.

"I feel all right," said Gabe, "except for these briars." He was just far enough back we could still hear him. When he caught up to us, he was pulling a string of saw briars loose from his shorts, carefully trying to unwind it. It was wrapped around him like a snake made of tire studs, ripping his bare legs something awful. It looked like someone had taken a small machine gun and pointed at him: rat-a-tat-tat across his legs, zigzagging back and forth. His legs looked pitiful. It is the only way to describe them. It hurt to see them.

The distance we'd traveled had been substantial. This trip was supposed to be a four to six-hour float. After hiking, climbing, falling, and fumbling for nearly three hard hours on Saturday evening and three more on Sunday morning, we'd covered maybe ten miles. We couldn't have much farther to go. It couldn't be more than just a mile or so to the end of the whitewater. But then what? That mile-and-a-half of river miles beyond the rapids might translate into five miles or more of climbing ridges to get out of the jungle. We might not make it out for another day. Thinking about the possibility of sleeping in another pile of leaves made me heartsick and thirsty. I didn't know about the others, but I knew I needed water.

"The next branch we come to let's get some water. It won't hurt us. We need it." I said, trying to sound enthusiastic.

"What about those amoebas and stuff?" Jack said. "Wild boars are supposed to carry some kind of viral infection which gives you diarrhea." But I wasn't worried. We needed water worse than the possibility of getting sick later.

Sammy added, "Out here, the streams are pretty clear and clean. It won't hurt us. We'll be drinking from spring-fed streams." A stomach infection wouldn't matter if we died of thirst first.

We spied a cool, little stream trickling down the next draw, a rocky brook. Just what the doctor ordered. Cupping my hand, I took a long drink. "Yaaaa!" I screamed out, the water stinging my throat. The pain surprised me. The water going down tasted good and cold, but it felt like a knife was being raked across the back of my throat. I drank all I wanted and then some. "Drink guys. We haven't had anything to drink at all since yesterday. You need to drink. We all do." But Jack wouldn't drink much. He took a little sip. I think he was worried about wild boar poop, and I don't blame him.

It was hard, boring traveling. We just marched, trudging through the kind of country you wouldn't dare hike through hunting wildflowers or game. It was straight up and down again, steep gorge country, the steepest yet. Silently, we marched through the forest like we had put ourselves on autopilot. We'd been at it maybe four hours again. The topography of this section was ridiculous, a thousand feet straight up vertically in six or seven-hundred yards. It was like climbing a mountain straight up or trying to walk out of a bucket.

Once or twice, we hiked a ridgeline for a quarter of a mile or more only to slide back down most of it. Sometimes we scampered up and then sat on our butts going down. As we did so, we rooted through rhododendron, tearing black loamy earth free, cutting a furrow as we went. We still couldn't see the real Abrams Creek. Then, suddenly, we'd turn and there it would be poking its head at us between trees. We'd snatch a glimpse of roaring whitewater and hear it, cuss it, then feel better knowing we were still on the right track.

In no time, we were warming to the sun, heating up. Though the day was still cool, we were sweating. It was arduous work plowing through this forest. We usually followed in Sammy's footsteps, though occasionally I would lead for a short stretch. The deafening roar from the water wasn't so great now, I was thinking. Looking up, straining to see Sammy, I thought I could see where the rapids gave way to calmer water. About this same instant, I was awakened from my daydreaming by Sammy's scream. "Yaaaiiiaaay!" "Yaaaiiiaaay!" Heeeeey?!?!"

Petrified, I looked up through the woods thirty yards ahead to where Sammy was supposed to be. I couldn't see him. It scared me. "Oh no," I thought. "Something has happened to Sammy." It wasn't odd that I couldn't see Sammy. Most of the time, I couldn't. Rarely could I see Jack. Occasionally, walking along, one of us would catch a glimpse of another. Somehow, it was just easier and more bearable to walk alone in the woods, near each other but alone.

Now Jack and Gabe were within sound distance of us, too, and could hear what I heard. We were all terrified by the emotion conveyed in Sammy's screams. He sounded like a desperate madman, a wounded animal. We couldn't see him. Lunging ahead ten or fifteen yards, I flew through a steep, nearly straight-down slice of gorge terrain toward the creek. It looked like calm water. I could see where the whitewater ended. This must be the embayment, I thought. Suddenly, Sammy screamed again, "HEEEEEY!" It was all happening so fast.

The next instant, a flash sent a cold chill through my body. It wasn't caused by the frenzy with which Sammy bolted through the forest like he was being chased by some enemy in an Asian war. It was another image. I saw it where the whitewater met the calm water, something so fantastic my eyes had trouble communicating to my brain. There was something blue down there below the whitewater in the lake. It's a boat! Boom! I took off screaming and hollering down the slope.

"HEEEEYYYY!!!!" I screamed. Sammy was far ahead, maybe eighty yards, halfway between me and the boat. "It can't leave us, it just can't," I thought. "We've got to make him hear us," is all I could think about. "HEEELLLLLP!" I screamed as I careened down the mountain, running as fast as I could: bounding and bouncing; brushing through hemlocks, pines, and laurel; heading down the mountain at a wicked angle, covering as much ground as possible.

I screamed again, although I realized Sammy was much closer than I was. My mind was racing: "He can't leave before we get there! What if he won't take us out? Who is it? He probably thinks were crazy. We're screaming; he might think we're gonna kill him. Oh please, God, we're not going to kill him! Let him be there. Let him know we're not going to kill him. Help us!"

There were a thousand prayers and questions racing through my mind. My body was tingling I was so excited and thrilled. Then, it hit me. Maybe we won't have to climb out. By the time I got about forty yards downstream I could see Sammy. He was standing near what appeared to be a blue boat. I could hear him talking to somebody.

I could see well enough through the underbrush to make out a luscious, spectacular scene. There was a beautiful deep azure pool where the tumultuous river poured into the embayment. It was the mouth of the stream where the whitewater crashed into a breathtakingly beautiful, swirling turmoil, its last lunge downward before it gave itself up to become a lake. It made for an unforgettable image. It looked like a holy place, a sacred place, maybe once used by Native Americans. Anyway, it seemed like a sacred place to me.

Inside the blue boat, which was struggling in the dangerous waters at the foot of the falls, I could make out a dog, a black Labrador. There were fishing poles all over the boat and an angel standing there. I could see him—or it. I don't know which it was. He was moving slowly, carefully maneuvering his boat, holding it steady in the swift, dangerous currents at the foot of the rapids. He was keeping the boat close to where I would be coming out of the rhododendron.

I was twenty or thirty feet above the scene. He must be able to see me, I thought. I couldn't see him clearly, and the boat kept moving away from the falls, somewhere to my left below. Then, I couldn't see the boat. It was blocked by rough rhododendron thickets. I really believed the driver of the boat was an angel. "Oh, no," I thought, "The blue boat is no longer in sight. But it doesn't matter; I know it's there. I can hear voices."

The rough trail Sammy tore open looked like it had been made by buffalo. It was that big and ended abruptly at a rock. Then, it began again on the other side of a short chasm. You had to go around this gap of maybe ten feet, because it was too far to jump. The trouble was that the bank on the left, the only way to get around it, had a steep rock face nearly straight up and down. Lunging and moving as hard as I could, I ran right around the edge of the bluff like a bicyclist in a bowl. I just ran and jumped through it. Coming to the final bit of overgrowth, I could make out the sound of a trolling motor. And I could see a Labrador retriever sitting in a boat at the foot of the falls next to an angel with a fishing pole.

There was blue outdoor carpet under my dirty, beat-up tennis shoes as I stepped onto the boat and collapsed cross-legged upon its deck. Looking up, I could see the dog smiling at me. The big Lab was smart enough to stick close to his master, who was busy navigating the boat downstream to pick up Sammy. I had come through the rhododendron closer to the boat than Sammy. I looked at all the fishing gear and thought, "Well, we've spoiled his fishing trip." I apologized to him. "Were you catching anything?" I asked.

"Just got here, just this minute got the poles out. This is a good place for smallmouth, here."

I felt a bit dizzy as the boat wafted and lunged back and forth in the turbulent fast water at the foot of the rapids where the man and his dog had come to fish this Sunday morning. Instead of catching smallmouth, the man (or angel or whatever he was) caught us. A fisher of men he was that day.

It took Jack and Gabe about ten minutes to catch up with us. Every few minutes, Jack would stick his head up out of the rhododendron. He had a big, broad smile on his face. It was wonderful to see him smiling, the first smile I'd seen since we left the fire that morning. Then, a moment later, Gabe would stick his head up, grinning ear to ear. They kept doing it, making sure we were still there and not leaving without them. They continued this routine until they reached the boat and got aboard.

The man worked carefully turning the boat around. It was full, and these were dangerous waters. His name was Mr. Campbell—Don, or Dan, I can't remember which. He said he lived just off 411, outside Maryville. He gave us some coffee from his thermos bottle. Unbelievable! We all had a long sip. It tasted so good. He even had cream and sugar, just the way I like it. Then, he offered us a giant Butterfinger candy bar, which we fought over! No, we didn't really; we shared it equally.

The sun was high now as we drifted into calmer water. It was a strange and exhilarating feeling, being driven downstream toward home by this good man. Where had he come from? How had he come to be here, and why? He said he was just out fishing. It was a good thing we were near the river, or we never would have seen him. Jack was right, after all.

As we motored away from Abrams Creek toward our car, many things went through our minds. On our left, out of the shadows as the sun rose high, we passed by a large stream. It was the foreboding mouth of Panther Creek. Seeing it from the boat, it was much larger than we anticipated. Crossing it would have been a monumental problem. If we hadn't been rescued, we would have had to swim it. That's one problem we didn't have to face.

Mr. Campbell no longer feared hitting his propeller on the bottom rocks below, so he started his motor, opening up the little boat. The waters deepened and widened to nearly two-hundred feet across. We were in open water now, moving along toward home. The wind felt good on our faces. "Look there!" someone yelled out as an osprey flew right over our heads, heading upstream toward the mountains. It was a sign, a good sign, for sure. Perhaps it was a Native American spirit signaling adieu to us, or possibly good riddance, who knows for sure.

It was an omen of some kind, a reminder not to forget this hard lesson, to revere this place and to pay it more respect next time. You can bet this river taught us new humility at nearly a terrible price. Maybe having this experience and managing to survive it with Jack and Gabe might help save their lives next time. Hopefully, they have learned something and won't take similar risks with their children's lives. We were lucky we weren't killed.

As we approached the bridge, we saw something bobbing up and down in the water. It was Sammy's little cooler. It had washed down from the rapids all the way through the embayment and found its way to the bridge and our parked car. There was no sign, though, of any of the rest of our gear: canoes, fishing poles, clothes. None of it was anywhere to be found.

We also saw a park ranger heading down the gravel ramp towards us. Squinting in the sun, he shielded his eyes, looked hard at us, and said something I couldn't hear. But Sammy responded from the front end of the boat. The ranger turned and walked up the ramp to use the phone in his car. Immediately, he notified our wives and Gabe's mom that we'd been found.

Our angel, Mr. Campbell, wouldn't take any money for helping us. I didn't think he would, but we felt obliged to make the offer, hoping it wouldn't offend him. He wouldn't even let us buy him coffee and another candy bar. He just turned and headed his boat back toward Abrams Creek with his dog at his side. He did wave at us, though, just an East Tennessean, a transplanted son of Scotland, Don Campbell or Dan Campbell, I never knew which.

Later, I tried calling all the Campbells in the Blount County and Maryville telephone directory, but none had ever heard of him. For some reason, I never could find Mr. Campbell to thank him for saving us. It's for this reason and others that I've never been sure whether Mr. Campbell might actually have been an angel. I really don't know.

The Abrams Creek Ranger Station sits in a small field sixty yards from the creek, about four hundred yards or so inside the National Park, right near the campground where we put in. When we got out of the car and walked up to the station, five big, somber-looking rangers were waiting for us. However, they did almost smile as we sheepishly approached. We must have looked like four bedraggled prodigal sons.

The area looked like a truck lot, full of four-wheel drive vehicles. Most of the owners were off duty. The "offs" had been called in because of us. It was a humbling experience approaching Mike Farley, Supervisor of Abrams Creek Ranger Station. We were bruised, exhausted, humiliated, hungry, and hurting. Mike stepped up and asked, "Are you guys all right? Is anybody hurt?"

"Yeah, we're fine. Glad to be alive. Glad to be out of there." We apologized profusely for costing them a night's sleep hunting for us. There was a yellow and orange fun yak, all shiny and glistening, laying conspicuously in the front yard. A fun yak is an air-filled, sturdy rubber kayak, large enough for two paddlers and an injured person. It can carry out a wounded soldier lying down, if necessary. Ranger Steve Kloster had brought it. "If you hadn't got out by eleven o'clock, we were going to use it and go in to get you," he said.

Ranger Farley explained what had happened throughout the night when he had been on the phone with our wives and Gabe's mom. They talked at 11:30 p.m., 1:30 a.m., 6:00 a.m., and 9:30 a.m. These men often deal with distraught and frightened people, not to mention lost and careless public visitors. They do it with a calm, usually caring attitude and professionalism. I wished we were meeting these good men under better circumstances. They had already called our families and told them we'd be home soon, and we'd probably want a big Sunday dinner.

I felt pretty stupid, but humility is a good thing. You don't make as many mistakes when you're humble. We were grateful for many things, mostly because we were safe. The rangers kept asking us how we felt. "Are you dizzy? Any bruises?" They bandaged the cut over Sammy's eye, and they looked at my hand and finger. Mike Farley said, "Your wedding ring might have to be cut off, or your finger. You better get that done pretty quickly, or you might lose the circulation in your finger." No one was seriously hurt, although I believe we were in shock. We also talked about hypothermia, one of the foremost dangers we faced, according to them.

Our world had shrunk these last two days. It was very strange for us to have spent so long on the edge where everything existed immediately—"no tomorrow," so to speak. For those last hours, the moment had been all the reality we knew: the moment we climbed the hill, swam for the canoe, pulled the rope to secure the boat. These actions—in fact, all our actions—were reduced by our circumstances to a base animal existence. All that mattered was to survive, action and reaction. Whether they turned out right or wrong, we had to live with them and their consequences.

So here we were, standing in front of those responsible for overseeing the safety of the Park's visitors. We had gotten ourselves into trouble, and we were fortunate to be standing at all to face the music. We were to blame. But the point here is this: it does not matter. We didn't do it on purpose, and we did our best to get out of there on our own. We just couldn't do it.

Perhaps, experiencing this immediacy of life, this heightened, exaggerated existence, is the most valuable experience we took away from our Great River Adventure. The lesson we learned is this: every action is important. Each moment of life, each choice we make is important. Make them count. In a lifetime in which it is possible to do good and right, do it. Make life matter.

"Sorry for costing you all a night's sleep," I said to them again, lamely. "That's all right. Think nothing of it!" is what I hoped I would hear back. But I didn't. I wanted to be let off the hook, consoled, pampered, and babied. We know the rangers were glad we were safe. But they also wanted us to understand the predicament we had put ourselves in and the expense and inconvenience we caused others. What they said was straightforward: "This is part of our jobs. You gave a lot of people quite a scare. You know better." There it is. We should have known better.

Sammy and I felt pretty bad. Our pride was hurt, and we were embarrassed to have all these people here because of our stupidity and hard-headedness. As Mike spoke, another pick-up truck arrived with "John Hicks, Contractor" painted on its side. John is a part-time volunteer working on kayak and whitewater rescues. He's also an avid fisherman and whitewater enthusiast. He was here waiting on a friend, and together they were planning on kayaking Abrams to rescue us if necessary. He volunteered to try to recover our boats and gear.

We thanked the rangers profusely, promised to get our bruises checked at the hospital, and departed in a manner similar to the crab moving backwards in T. S. Eliot's poem "The Love Song of J. Alfred Prufrock"—"scuttling across the floors of silent seas."

As we slowly headed out of the mountains, things that once bothered us didn't anymore, at least for now. Mundane responsibilities like returning a rented canoe just didn't seem to matter. We didn't even know if the canoe existed any longer. And what's more, we didn't care. With this goofy, devil-may-care attitude, we arrived at Shoney's to eat, and we killed them at the Shoney's breakfast bar. What exactly we ate, I don't remember. But we ate a lot of it. We drank orange juice, water, and coffee, too, and then more water and coffee. We were dirty and must have smelled like the underside of a hank—a side of smoked bacon. It had been over twenty-four hours since our last meal. So, we just sat down amidst the church crowd and feasted, eating everything we could get our hands on, anything we could find, and we found a lot.

While we were eating, Sammy mentioned something about his throat being sore. "Yeah, my throat's sore, too," Jack added. Mine hurt, and so did Gabe's. It was the first time we were all aware that we suffered from the same ailment, the same discomfort. None of us knew what caused it, or why it was common to all of us. Later, at the doctor's office, we learned our throat problems were caused by exposure to the cold, dehydration, and exhaustion. None of us had experienced it before, and none of us have since.

Lynnie met Jack and me with hugs and kisses when we got home. She took it all well. I thought she would be angry, but she was past that stage. Sammy and Gabe each drove home by themselves. Jack and I showered and slept until about four p.m., when Jack got up and ate again. I went down to the emergency room at the hospital, where they charged me $285 to x-ray my hand, cut my wedding ring off, and tell me I had a hairline fracture. There was nothing much they could do for it except wrap it.

I was also given a good physical check-up and felt like it alone might be worth $285. But, of course, I didn't have any idea what I was being charged at the time, nor did I care. I was hurting right then. I didn't get the bill until later, and I was hurting then, too. Mr. Torance Popejoy, a farmer neighbor of mine, would have cut my ring off for free with a pair of tinsnips, if only I'd asked him.

Later that night, I received a call from John Hicks and his partner. They said, "We had a hair-raising ride down Abrams Creek trying to locate your boats. One boat is okay," he reported. "We pulled it out on the bank. It looked like two of the fishing poles were all right. But we couldn't get anything else out. The water was too high and wild. The best we could do was to pull the gear out of it and put it up on the bank."

I asked him about Sammy's boat. He'd found it. "The other boat is pretty well trashed," he said. "Both thwarts are broken, and there's a big dent in its side. It's lodged under some timber. You'd have to have a saw to get it out."

Two days later and with no rain, two different river enthusiasts mounted another expedition. They did recover the rented canoe and my fishing poles, but one of the reels had been destroyed. I went to get them late Tuesday night. The reel was a pitiful looking bird's nest of knotted fishing line with sprigs of rhododendron.

With the assistance of the staff at Riversports, we contacted two other whitewater enthusiasts to try again to retrieve Sammy's boat. Four days and no rain later, a third expedition and rescue party went down Abrams Creek with a saw to cut Sammy's boat loose. Finally, five days after we had tried to go smallmouth fishing on Abrams Creek and never even wet a line, Sammy's boat was ridden out with a kayak inside of it. According to John Hicks, "in these circumstances, with such ferocious water levels, this maneuver is extremely dangerous."

John Malloy, a local whitewater enthusiast and outdoor writer, who was out of town at the time of our trip, told me later, "The day you ran the river at Abrams Creek, the water gauge at Little River was running extremely high." This gauge serves as a barometer for most backcountry streams. It measures water flow in cubic feet per second (CFS). For ideal smallmouth bass fishing on a lazy float, we found out it should ideally be running between 400 and 1,400 CFS. The day we got into trouble on our float down Abrams Creek, it was running at 14,000 to 15,000 CFS. That's fourteen or fifteen times what is regarded as ideal and safe. Yikes! We should have been killed.

My first night home after our adventure, I awoke in terrific pain. The clock read 3:50 a.m. I've never been in a plane crash, but I felt like I'd just crawled out from one. Somehow, I managed to make it downstairs and took a hot bath. The muscles in my legs hurt so badly I didn't think I could walk. It was the muscle that wraps around both knees and meets in the groin. I couldn't get in and out of a car without severe pain for two or three weeks. I'd been going to the YMCA for the last three months and thought I was in pretty good shape, but I was wrong. Four days after the adventure, I still hurt so badly I went to the YMCA to have a massage. I was still in enough pain I was willing to do anything for relief, go to any lengths. It was like the old football playing days. I soaked in the whirlpool, and my muscles relaxed some, but they didn't cease aching for a long time.

Sammy said he didn't go to the hospital until the second day after we returned. Throughout the first night, his knee caused him so much pain he put ice on it all night. By morning, it still hurt so badly he soaked in a hot tub for almost an hour, just like I did. We figured we were both in our tubs at four a.m. that morning. He went to the emergency room the second day for x-rays. He found out his knee was severely bruised, but there was no permanent cartilage or ligament damage.

While I was getting x-rayed, I asked the doctor about the severity of my pain. "It's your age," he said.

"It's my age? I'm only forty-four years old and in pretty good health. What's the matter with me? I feel like I've been in a plane wreck."

The doctor said, "For each decade over twenty years of age, it takes you another day before you peak in the amount of pain you feel."

Gabe and Jack were fine. Jack was a little sore the next day. When Gabe got back home on Sunday he cut the grass. That's how sore and tired he was from the Great Adventure. His scratches healed quickly, as well. Two weeks after our trip, little cat-like white scratch lines were still visible on his legs, but that was all.

"Ah, youth." It was my father-in-law, Hal Jones, who explained it to me. When I told him about the boys and how much pain Sammy and I were still experiencing, he said, "You know how long it takes a fifteen-year-old to get rested?"

"I don't know," I said.

He laughed and said, "About an hour!" I guess he's right. It took Sammy and me a long, hard, painful month to heal.

It was a hot, sunny, lazy Sunday afternoon two months later in June before I could talk Lynnie into returning to Abrams Creek with me. As we drove up to the mountains, I explained my reason, "I just want to see the creek again." We parked in front of the put-in place where Jack and Gabe had fixed the fishing gear we never got to use. Lynnie walked up to the campground on the gravel road, while I just found a nice cool spot in the shade to sit and watch the creek.

That day, Abrams Creek looked like any lazy summer stream in the Great Smoky Mountains. It was barely more than a trickle. Tubing down it would have been difficult. The stream was too shallow, not enough rain. You'd have to drag or walk your inner tube along the slick bottom. But I could see a stretch or two around the bend where it might be a little deeper, a little swifter. It was hard to believe this creek could be so dangerous.

I'm blessed to have this chance to tell this little story. One day, maybe Jack or Gabe, or one of you who reads it, might pause to consider one of your decisions in the woods, on a creek, or in a river when others are depending on you. Maybe you'll remember our Great River Adventure and the mistakes we made. Perhaps you'll pause and reconsider one of your choices. Instead, take the smartest, safest, surest, shrewdest, and most careful and secure route. It will be the right choice in the long run, even if it takes you a little more time.

God protected me and mine on Abrams Creek that day in April 1994. I will do my best to remember it. I could have been punished for my sins of pride, impatience, foolhardiness, and impetuousness. The mountains are no place for these shortcomings.

Abrams Creek is still flowing and will always be flowing. The mountains, forests, and rivers of the Great Smoky Mountains give few people leeway to make the same mistake twice.

A Final Note

I wish to thank the GSMNP rangers who assisted in our April 1994 rescue, including rangers Mike Farley of Cades Cove District, Al Voner, Steve Kloster, and Todd Remaly, a seasonal ranger for the Park.

The official report refers to an "unnamed fisherman as coming

to the aid of the lost party on the lower end of Abrams Creek."
I know this fisherman to be either a man named Campbell who
lives outside of Maryville off Highway 411 or an angel sent from
heaven to save us. Perhaps they are one and the same.

According to Park records, between thirty to seventy search
and rescue missions occur each year in the Great Smoky Mountains National Park. They range from assisting an injured person
to looking for missing or overdue hikers. In 1993, for instance,
there were seventy-one rescue efforts, of which four were major
Park searches. The number of rescue personnel involved varies
but is usually between four and ten people per rescue. More ex-
tensive searches may involve as many as one-hundred personnel
and include paid technical assistance or specialized equipment.

Often, search efforts are to locate overdue hikers who are
between four or five hours late. Our rescue was a little more
complicated. Most typically begin with a hasty search where
the victims were last seen. The next stage often involves dogs
and helicopters. These Park employees do a tremendous job. It
would behoove visitors to be more aware of the job the GSMNP
rangers do in their rescue efforts, as well as the work they do in
protecting the nation's natural resources.

In 2007, I bought some land, built a cabin, and now live very
near where our adventure took place in the Smoky Mountains. I
don't know if this is to remind me of our near-death experience. I
can say that I have never again attempted to float Abrams Creek.

Bill's Little Stories:
Irrepressible Cussedness

The following is one of my favorite sayings
from Bodkins Treasury of Southern Folklore.
It refers to Davy Crockett, or any backwoods
frontiersman, whom we admire for laughing in
the face of adversity:

It is the most important characteristic of an
East Tennessean, the one that keeps only a very
few men from acknowledging defeat . . . When
the combination of adverse circumstances, at
last reaches such a place, a climax, where there
is no other choice but to go on, to take one
more step, then another.

And all the time, there he was playing
his tricks of making a way out of a 'no-way;'
of hitting a straight lick with a crooked stick,
winning the jack pot with no other stake but a
laugh; fighting a mighty battle without outside
showing force, and winning his war from
within.

Midway High School Graduation

From a speech for the May 17, 2010 commencement
at Midway High School in Roane County, Tennessee.

Congratulations! You are to be congratulated on your achievement. This is a momentous day in your lives. Thank you for inviting me to say a few words. Hopefully, these few words and thoughts, acquired during my sixty-plus years of living, will be of some help to you on your individual journeys after Midway. Life is a quest. You have made a great start, but your journey is just beginning.

Winston Churchill, Britain's great World War II Prime Minister, once gave a graduation speech where he stood up and said, "Never give up. Never give up. Never, ever give up." Then, he sat down.

At my graduation, we had a wonderful speaker who spoke exceedingly well, but I can't remember anything that he told us, only that he said it well.

The great writer, Kurt Vonnegut, who is the author of *Slaughterhouse-Five* and *Welcome to the Monkey House*, gave a pretty famous talk to a graduation class a few years ago. In it, he told the graduates to laugh, to dance often, to love, and love well; and a few other wonderful things that if practiced daily or often would improve life and make it better. My life experiences and time with so many great and wise Tennesseans have taught me much. Some of these valuable lessons and simple truths I'll try to share with you. They are but simple truths, but at the same time, they are not so simple after all.

1.   The most important thing to become a success in life is this: Dress up and show up. That is the key to success in life. Most people won't do it. Something will always

get in the way of just getting up every day and doing what they are supposed to do. Life is not a sprint; it's a long-distance race.

2. If you're gonna be dumb, you better be tough. That is, you can do it the easy way or the hard way. The easy way is better, usually. It's not so hard on you.

3. Do what you have to do first. Then, do what you should do. Then, do what you want to do.

4. Do the next right thing. When you don't know what else to do, and you will experience this many times in your life, then, just do the next right thing.

5. He, who smelt it, dealt it. That's another way of saying "the smeller's the feller."

6. You are never given anything you cannot bear. When things get tough, and they will, remember this.

7. Hard work always pays off. Maybe not today or tomorrow, or when you want it, but it always does.

8. What goes around comes around. There is such a thing as karma. You get back what you give out. The Beatles said it, too: "The love you take is equal to the love you make." Love well and often. (The next three are my mother's favorites.)

9. The road to hell is paved with good intentions.

10. If you can't say anything good about someone, don't say anything at all.

11. Never wake a sleeping baby.

12. Listen and remember what your parents taught you. You will need it every day of your life. Once, my father-in-law, Hal Jones, asked my son, Jack, how things were going. Jack was having trouble in graduate school, so, Hal said, "Well, you see the light at the end of the tunnel, don't you?" Jack sort of grimaced because he didn't. So Hal said, "Well, you see the tunnel, don't you?" The lesson here is sometimes you can't see the light at the end of the tunnel, but you CAN see the tunnel. Sometimes all you can do is put one foot in front of the other.

13. Mr. Cooper, the millstone sharpener from Rennie, Tennessee, asked me once if I'd ever seen anybody

sharpen a millstone before. When I told him I hadn't, he said, "There's a whole lot of things in this ole world that you don't know a thing about!" Ain't that right!

14. Your attitude is what's important. Smile; try to get along with your fellows. Most of the bad things in life that you are sure are going to happen don't materialize. Don't waste time worrying. Things are never as bad as they seem. Sometimes the hardest thing NOT to do is worry. Worrying is a waste of time; change your attitude instead.

15. Be careful what you wish for, you might get it. This includes jobs, wives, girlfriends, money, etc.

16. Don't worry about other people; you have no control over them. Keep your side of the street clean. Taking care of you is a full-time job.

17. Live each day as if it is your last. Live one day at a time. Seven miracles happen each day if you are aware enough to see them.

18. Be a good enough friend to allow people to help you. This is almost reverse selfishness. It's easy to give, isn't it? Be as good a getter as you are a giver. It's more difficult to allow other people the pleasure of giving to you! Allow people the joy of giving themselves to you.

19. The best you are ever going to do each day is to get up and fail, because you are human. Get up when you get knocked down. Dust yourself off. Try again. That's what life is all about.

20. The grass isn't greener on the other side of the hill. Make your own grass green. Don't waste time wishing you were someone else, or lived or worked somewhere else, were married to someone else. Live your life; it is here and now. Live it.

21. When a door closes another opens. You've got to do something. Plant a tree. Feed the birds. It's not always about you. We are put here to work. Don't wait until it's too late. Do it now. Rely on other people. Ask for help. This self-sufficiency stuff is a lot of crap.

22. Remember the golden rule and practice it every day: Do unto others as you'd have them do unto you.

23. Keep your powder dry; sharpen your axes and your mind. Shine your shoes. Wash your hands and blow your nose. Drink milk, eat pork, and drink lots of water. Be prepared.

24. All it takes is a pocket knife to carve soapstone, a worm to catch a fish, a loose word to sink a ship, or a candle to light the darkness.

25. When the dogwoods bloom, go fishing. Then, when the mayflies hatch, go fishing, too.

26. Always keep your promises.

27. Help the downtrodden, feed the hungry, encourage the young.

28. Pray every day.

29. Have fun. But, remember, nothing good happens after midnight.

30. The most important thing is family. Charity begins at home.

31. Think before you speak. Back up what you say.

32. Save for a rainy day—you never know when you'll need it.

33. Lefty loosey, tighty righty.

34. My last thought is one of my mother's, as well. Pride comes before the fall. So live. Live on. Love. Love well and often. Dance as much as you can. Laugh loud and often, and be a good friend.

Good luck.

Coda

Hopefully, you've enjoyed this book. It may not be my last. What new adventures and stories life has in store, one can only wonder. After a nice rest, like Bilbo Baggins, I'll be off again on some grand new adventure – maybe, not so grand.

How about you? I look forward to sharing stories with you again. Until then, like Herb Trentham said:

> While ago's done gone.
> We ain't got no promise of a directly.
> All we got's rite now.
> Don't spile this day.

See you on the reruns. Adieu!
I better go look for my dog Buddy!

Sincerely,

Bill

Credits and Acknowledgments

The Spartans of Rhea County: Photos of two of the Spartans (Barbara Allen and Rhoda Tennessee Thomison) courtesy of Debbie Moore, from 1911 publication of an article written by G. Allen in Volume 19 of *Confederate Veterans Magazine.* Photos of the Chattanooga Bluffs, originally from the Chattanooga Public Library Archives, and Moccasin Bend, originally from the TVA Archives, are from Bill Landry's collection.

Buddy: Dog of the Smoky Mountains: Emails about Buddy courtesy of J.D. Schandt, Hunter Foreman, and Jan Kelly. All photos of Buddy are courtesy of Katie Folen, except for "J. D.'s photo of Buddy" provided by J. D. Schandt, and "Buddy in sun on Little Bottom Trail" provided by Jan Kelly. The photo of the otter is courtesy of Great Smoky Mountains National Park Wildlife Services.

The Tomato War: Photos courtesy of Ken Coffey, Grainger County Historian, with special thanks to Grainger Today for use of photos by Ann Cason. Thanks to Bobby Longmire for recreating the tomato war shield graphic.

Over Home in Hancock County: All photos courtesy of Linda and Jerry Burke, except for the photo of "Cecile Turner by clean, pure headwaters of the Clinch River," provided by the Charles Turner family, and "Coy Collins" provided by his son Scotty Collins.

Old Balsam: Elk photos courtesy of the Great Smoky Mountains National Park Wildlife Services. "An early snow" is courtesy of Katie Folen. The photo of Cataloochie Church is courtesy of Frank Norris.

The Ballad of Pirate Paddy O'Dea: Cartoon drawing courtesy of Ryan Webb.

Reed and Creed Kirkland: All family photos of Reed and Creed Kirkland courtesy of Creed Kirkland. "Bears in tree" and "Skinning bears" courtesy of Jerry Hughes.

Mountain Speech: Photos of Black Will Walker, Jack Huff, and Lucinda Oakley Ogle are courtesy of the Great Smoky Mountains National Park Archives. Photo of Maynard Ledbetter is courtesy of Inez "Granny" Adams. Photo of

Mann Ledbetter and the hunters is used courtesy of the Bill Landry collection.

The Harlequin Massacre: Photos of the Harlequins in performance courtesy of Dr. Jim Lewis, with special thanks to Mac Smotherman, Chairman, Theater Department, University of Tennessee at Chattanooga.

Charlie Garland's Stove: Photo by Frank Norris courtesy of Great Smoky Mountains Heritage Center, Townsend. Photo of Jim and Jake Garland courtesy of the Garland family.

The Great River Adventure: Photos of Abrams Creek in snow and Abrams bridge courtesy of Katie Folen. Photos of Abrams Creek steep banks, bald eagle, and Abrams after 2012 tornado courtesy of Frank Norris. The hog and bear photos are courtesy of the Great Smoky Mountains National Park Archives. Typical stream flow, sunlight through trees, cathedral wilderness, typical side branch photo, and green mansions surround us are courtesy of Steve Moore. Sammy and Bill photo courtesy of the Bill Landry collection. Gabe and Jack photo courtesy of Lynn Landry.

Thanks to cartographer Neil Smith for the East Tennessee area map and the Civil War map in "The Spartans of Rhea County."

Thanks to Dr. Bethany Dumas, Laura Armour, Betty Best, Mary Lynn Gilmore, and Laura Fry for their help reading and editing the manuscript. Any errors are mine. Special thanks to Sam Venable, my friend and partner on the "Talk is Cheap Tour," for his notes on the hardcopy edition book jacket.

About the Author

Bill Landry is the voice, host, narrator, and co-producer of *The Heartland Series*, which has aired on WBIR-TV for nearly thirty years. Since its beginnings in 1984, over 1,900 short features have been produced, including 150 half-hour specials. Bill has written, produced, and acted in many of the episodes.

Receiving an MFA from Trinity University at the Dallas Theater Center and a BA in literature from the University of Tennessee at Chattanooga, Bill has gone on to receive two Emmy Awards for directing *The Heartland Series*, the Education in Appalachia Award from Carson-Newman University, and an Honorary Doctorate in Humanities from Lincoln Memorial University.

For over thirty years Bill has written, produced, and performed his one-man play, *Einstein the Man*. He has presented the play over 1,000 times in thirty-eight states and two provinces of Canada. In 2000, the script was distributed by the Tennessee Department of Education. In 2003, Bill's production of *The George Washington Carver Project* was distributed statewide, as well.

In 2009, Bill premiered his DVD production of *William Bartram – An Unlikely Explorer* for the seventy-fifth anniversary of the founding of The Great Smoky Mountain National Park, which tells the tale of the little known eighteenth-century explorer, adventurer, and naturalist.

Deeply rooted in the Appalachian region, Bill has served on the boards of Fish Hospitality Pantries, Beck Cultural Exchange, the Clarence Brown Theater, the Princess Theater Foundation in Harriman, and the Sequoyah Birthplace Museum in Vonore, Tennessee. In 2011, his book, *Appalachian Tales & Heartland Adventures* was published by Celtic Cat Publishing, and is now in its third printing.

In 2011, Governor Bill Haslam appointed Bill to the Tennessee Historical Commission.

Bill works as a spokesman for WBIR-TV and for several other companies including Hallsdale Powell Utility District. He continues to write, direct, and produce video documentaries, and gives lectures and speeches, including his popular presentations of "An Evening with Bill Landry."

About Celtic Cat Publishing

Celtic Cat Publishing was founded in 1995 to publish emerging and established writers. The following works are available from Celtic Cat Publishing at *www.celticcatpublishing.net, Amazon.com*, and major bookstores.

Regional	*Appalachian Tales & Heartland Adventures*, Bill Landry *Tellin' It for the Truth*, Bill Landry
Poetry	*The Ghost in the Word: Poems*, Arthur J. Stewart *Exile Revisited*, James B. Johnston *Revelations: Poems*, Ted Olson *Marginal Notes*, Frank Jamison *Rough Ascension and Other Poems of Science*, Arthur J. Stewart *Bushido: The Virtues of Rei and Makoto*, Arthur J. Stewart *Circle, Turtle, Ashes*, Arthur J. Stewart *Ebbing & Flowing Springs*, Jeff Daniel Marion *Gathering Stones*, KB Ballentine *Fragments of Light*, KB Ballentine *Guardians*, Laura Still
Fiction	*The Price of Peace*, James B. Johnston *Outpost Scotland*, Abbott A. Brayton *Fast Moving Cows and Other Tales*, Pat Magee
Humor	*Life Among the Lilliputians*, Judy Lockhart DiGregorio *Memories of a Loose Woman*, Judy Lockhart DiGregorio *Jest Judy* (CD), Judy Lockhart DiGregorio
Chanukah	*One for Each Night: Chanukah Tales and Recipes*, Marilyn Kallet
Young Adult	*Voyage of Dreams: An Irish Memory*, Kathleen E. Fearing
Children	*The Christmas Tree Angel*, Lisa Soland *Buddy: Dog of the Smoky Mountains*, Ryan Webb and Sharon Poole *Jack the Healing Cat* (English), Marilyn Kallet *Jacques le chat guérisseur* (French), Marilyn Kallet *Twins*, Tracy Ryder Bradshaw
Memoir	*Being Alive*, Raymond Johnston
Philosophy	*The Epiphany of K*, Kenneth Godwin